Y0-AAC-185

WHAT REVIEWERS SAY ABOUT

MASTERING INTERNETWORKING

"[The] **highly readable style** was enjoyable and the insights informative...Keep up the good work of addressing an often misunderstood arena of communications technology."

—Harrell Van Norman, consultant/author in network performance and optimization

"An **exceptionally good** study guide that will enable the earnest student to firmly grasp the complexities of LAN internetworking. Upon completion of this series, the network manager should be able to cut through vendor hoopla and cull the most salient information necessary to successfully build a corporate internetwork."

—Maureen Molloy, Network World

"...**communicates concepts extremely well**. Takes a **real-world**, hands-on approach." **Rated A** (= excellent)

—Computer Book Review

"**Invaluable**! A sure-fire winner with other working network managers, here and elsewhere in Europe."

—E. C., Network Manager, Dublin Ireland

"I can understand internetworking now! Thank you for producing something **readable**, that doesn't talk down to me. For someone in voice comm, making the transition to data comm manager has been hard...**this makes it easy**."

—InternationalTelecom Manager, SFSU Extension participant

"**Best of the lot**—and I've read a lot!...eminently readable and the material is accurate, **especially good in bridging and routing**...Can't wait to see Advanced Internetworking"

—Sadie Lewis, voice/data network consultant

"**Well-done**, almost effortless learning, written simply, light of jargon, with **terms clearly defined** as they come up. The information is all there, most often graphically depicted. It is also **instructionally sound**—it starts with review of the basics and gradually builds new information on what has already been clearly presented."

—Rita Lewis, Instructional Designer

"Now there's a middle ground [between live training and consultants]: a self learning guide that **allows net managers to go at their own pace** and ask questions about their networks along the way.... The exams at the end of each chapter take some unusual forms, from internetwork design projects to crossword puzzles."

—Data Communications Magazine

Mastering Internetworking

Self-Paced Learning Series

V.C. Marney-Petix

Numidia Press
Fremont, CA 94536

Mastering Internetworking

Self-Paced Learning Series

Supervising Editors: Amy Falkowitz and Valerie Matsumoto
Design, layout and illustrations by Dawn Dombrow

Printed in the United States of America.

Library of Congress Cataloging-In-Publication Data

Marney-Petix, V. C. (Victoria C.)

Mastering Interntworking/V. C. Marney-Petix.

p. cm.

Includes bibliographical references and index.

ISBN 1-880548-04-6 $24.95

1.Computer networks. 2.Local area networks (Computer Networks) 3.Wide area networks (Computer Networks) I. Title.

TK5105.5.M3595 1992

004.6--dc20 91-44241

CIP

Table of Contents

Preface

Internetworking, even in the hands of the best teachers, remains a very complex subject. People who attend my live training classes spend an intensive day struggling with the basics of bridging, routing and tunnelling and truly deserve a pat on the back when they complete the day. Give yourself full accolades when you put your pen down at the end of this self-paced learning as well.

This book and the live training program that preceded its creation were designed primarily for network managers and others who need to understand network technology so they can apply it to business problems. The straightforward technical tutorial breaks occasionally to allow you to complete checklists and apply the new information to your own network. I focus on constructing a strong conceptual framework for each subject and use the standards models as an anchor for understanding how all the complex material fits together.

I approached this book with the same underlying personal mission that animates me when teaching: I care deeply about the widespread confusion of terminology in vendor materials and want to bring a unifying perspective to the subject by defining terms and concepts in what I consider the "correct" way. For that reason, you may find some words defined somewhat differently here than you are used to. If completion of this training has made you a consumer who is simultaneously enthusiastic about potential benefits and wary about specific product claims and hype, I will have succeeded in my mission.

This book will take you on a tour of local (LAN), campus and wide-area (WAN) internets and their hardware and software components. Chapter 0 is a LAN review. Chapter 1 reviews the essentials of networking architectures by focusing on the Open Systems Interconnection (OSI) Model and its seven layers of functions. Even if you feel very familiar with basic networking, please at least skim this chapter because the remainder of the book assumes that you have mastered this material. Chapter 1 also introduces the beginning concepts of internetworking.

Chapter 2 focuses on repeaters and bridges, the Layers 1 and 2 connection devices. In addition to a very full discussion of bridging algorithms and standards (Spanning Tree and Source Routing are highlighted), you will take a close look at the kinds of applications that should use bridges. Smart bridges and other turbo-charged Layer 2 devices are included in the bridge discussion.

In Chapter 3, you will focus on routers and gateways. Unfortunately, an entire book could be written on routing and this is only a beginning course on internetworking, so I've had to limit the discussion considerably. This chapter gives you a grounding in the "hot" routing issues, including the uses of multi-protocol routing and hybrid bridge/routers, and introduces Network Layer and Application Layer gateways, how they are used and the applications they are best suited for.

Chapters 2 and 3 primarily focused on LAN–LAN internetworking in a local, campus or metropolitan area. In Chapter 4, you will turn your attention to the transport technologies used in long-distance LAN–LAN and LAN–WAN internetworking. These transport technologies include packet- and circuit-switching, in both their traditional and state-of-the-art incarnations.

Chapter 5 focuses on management of a corporate internet, with attention to national and international management standards as well as the most common problem areas and how to proactively manage them. I should remind all my readers that the advice contained in this chapter is the best advice I can give on these subjects and corresponds to what I share with my consulting clients. I am not, however, infallible; I certainly have no knowledge of the details of your network topology and applications. Use your own best judgement in applying the lessons of this chapter.

Chapter 6 takes you into the future of internetworking solutions and is entirely composed of my personal (albeit well-experienced and informed) opinion on this subject. It also includes guidelines for planning your future education in networking. Appendix B lists many companies that provide products in the areas we've covered in the text. Contact them for product information when you are ready to consider specific purchases. Having completed this course, you will be in an excellent position to understand their sales materials.

I recommend that you work your way through the entire book, from cover to cover, stinting no page and testing yourself honestly on the material in each chapter. Your eyes are not disceiving you; the comprehensive final exam is a crossword puzzle. Go ahead and try it! When you have completed the learning phase of using this book, apply the decision-tools to your business.

This book is only an introduction to the wonderful world of internetworking. When you are ready to build on what you have learned, do continue with *Mastering Advanced Internetworking* and *Mastering Network Management.*

Victoria Marney-Petix

Acknowledgements

Three groups of people have made this book project possible. Group 1 is a team of wonderful, generous techies. The technical people who have shared their knowledge with me over the years were augmented by a proof-reading team from Cisco, 3Com, Hughes LAN Systems, Network General, BT North America, Hewlett-Packard, Apple and Network Equipment Technologies. Ellen Brigham and Ron Kowalka were especially generous with their expertise. Group 2 is the team of trainers who hammered on me for all my pedagogical flaws. I especially thank Sandrella Robinson, wielder of the biggest hammer. (She is now East Coast Marketing Director for Numidia Press.) Thank you all so much!

The most important of these groups is the last on the list: the earnestly-striving, hard-working professionals who have taken time from their work-week or their weekend (oh, those sunny Saturdays) to learn and grow in their knowledge of internetworking with me for the last 6 years. Every confusion you experienced, every suggestion you made, every request for additional information—all your enthusiasm and love for the subject—has made this course better every time I teach it. It is now what it always has been: the best that I can do. All remaining flaws, whether technical or otherwise, are entirely my own fault.

Other people outside of these groups contributed the additional glue that kept me going to the finish line. Valerie Matsumoto, Ph.D., Editor and F.F. (Fabulous Friend), is at the top of this list. Over the past 15 years I've stolen all of her great teaching techniques and leaned on her unmercifully for advice prior to all my personal and business decisions. The smart moves were her ideas; the hair-brained remainder were my unique contribution to the partnership. Everybody needs a smart, innovative, funny and generous best friend; only a few of us are so blessed.

My spouse of a zillion years, James Marney-Petix, said to me, at least one night a week: "Go on back to the office and work on your book, dear. I'll take care of things at home." Greater love hath no person than to change 21 litter boxes when it's not their chores night.

My mother-by-adoption, Elizabeth Pearson, gave me my first education in internetworking. She has spent the last 25 years acting as a human bridge, gently helping diverse groups of people to understand and appreciate each other despite the laundry list of incompatibilities humans are capable of creating for themselves. On a personal level, she has offered me a living model of the difference between "I can't" and "It'll be difficult" when ethical decisions need to be made. I have tried.

Finally, I want to thank Joan Simien, who never loses hope in eventual personal victory for herself and everyone around her, spreads her generosity of spirit like a cloak, covering up all the imperfections beneath, and is, through it all, one hell of a good business manager and publisher. I can't wait to start on the next project!

Victoria Marney-Petix

Dedication

Elizabeth J. Pearson

and

James R. Marney-Petix

0

Reviewing LAN Technology

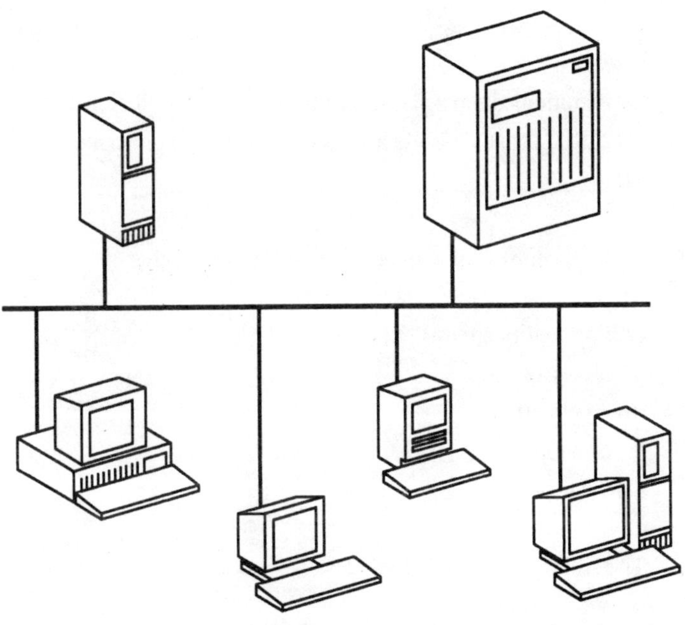

Before you proceed into the body of this book, take the time (about 30 minutes) to work your way through this review of basic local area network (LAN) technology. This book assumes that you are very proficient in basic LAN technology and architecture and does not review these subjects very extensively. These questions were taken from the comprehensive review at the end of *Mastering LAN Enabling Technologies*.

1. Token-passing is a(n):
   (a) topology
   (b) access method
   (c) medium
   (d) architecture

2. CSMA/CD means:
   (a) connection service management architecture with collision detection
   (b) communication sense multiple access with collision detection
   (c) carrier sense multiple access with corporate discount
   (d) ________________________________

3. Name the OSI layers, in order from lower to higher

4. OSI's "quality control" Layer is:
   (a) Network
   (b) Application
   (c) Session
   (d) Transport

5. The Application Layer includes:
   (a) WordPerfect 5
   (b) DbaseIII
   (c) X.400
   (d) all of the above

6. Connectionless transport means:
   (a) datagrams
   (b) micro-to-mainframe
   (c) virtual circuits

(d) multiplexing allowed

7. An application that uses an entirely datagram network:
   (a) electronic mail
   (b) loan approval (FHA)
   (c) retail credit approval (Visa)
   (d) modelling and CAD/CAM

8. The most popular medium for new LAN installations in offices is:
   (a) structured wiring or shielded twisted pair
   (b) unshielded twisted pair
   (c) IBM Token Ring
   (d) optical fiber

9. The star topology:
   (a) is the underlying physical topology of 802.5 logical rings
   (b) can be used with UTP wiring
   (c) has a central point of failure
   (d) all of the above

10. The 802 committee is involved in ________ standards.
    (a) LAN wiring
    (b) LAN management
    (c) LAN/ISDN integration
    (d) LAN bridging
    (e) all of the above

11. You should connect ONLY _____ to a LAN backbone.
    (a) user devices with the same architecture
    (b) user devices with the same protocols
    (c) concentrators and connection infrastructure devices
    (d) wide area connection devices
    (e) high-bandwidth user devices

12. At least one statement below concerning TCP/IP is not true. Find the error(s).

    (a) originally developed for ARPANET, the Dept of Labor network

    (b) a full stack, from Physical to Application Layers

    (c) has an Application Layer protocol called Telenet

    (d) will eventually outcompete OSI protocols, especially in Canada

13. Unshielded twisted pair can (in 1992) support 10BaseT:

    (a) only when connecting concentrators to a backbone

    (b) on runs up to 100 meters only

    (c) on runs of up to 15 kilometers with repeaters

    (d) only in OSI installations, with other protocols you must use fiber

14. Fiber optic cable is particularly important as a backbone medium. For which application would you be most likely to choose fiber to the desktop:

    (a) retail loan department, local branch, Durango Bank

    (b) electronic mail, Foremost-McKesson Foods

    (c) "Star Wars" systems development, CIA HQ

    (d) file sharing and database access, department LAN, The Limited

15. Novell's Network and Transport Layer protocols were derived from the ________ architecture.

    (a) XNS

    (b) OSI

    (c) TCP/IP

    (d) UtahNet, a proprietary early protocol stack

16. The process of standardization has followed which pattern:

    (a) software, hardware, applications

    (b) applications, transport, MIS job titles

    (c) hardware, connectivity software, transport software, applications support

    (d) interfaces, protocols, communications, remote modems

17. A protocol analyzer can:

    (a) transparently change Ethernet packets into token ring packets

    (b) read sender and destination addresses only

    (c) change an 802.3 to an Ethernet packet and back, to comply with standards

    (d) read both addresses and user data from a packet

    (e) change 802.3 packets into 802.5 packets, but there is a performance "hit"

18. The MOST IMPORTANT reason buyers are migrating to intelligent hubs is because they (are):

    (a) cheaper than passive hubs

    (b) cheaper than hubless network wiring

    (c) more manageable

    (d) deliver faster end-to-end user connections than hubless or passively hubbed networks

19. Define the following:

    FDDI

    Ethernet

    802.5

    coaxial cable

20. List two advantages of standards for USERS.

21. List two advantages of standards for VENDORS.
22. The LAN operating system (NOS) with the largest market share (1992) is:

    (a) SNA and SAA

    (b) Vines

    (c) LAN Manager

    (d) NetWare

23. To send a packet to another user on the same LAN, your interface software needs to know the other device/user's:

    (a) log-on name or alias

    (b) data link address

    (c) network address

    (d) both data link and network address

24. Define the following:

    drop cable

    transceiver

    STP

    UTP

25. For sales reps:

    One of your customers, a network manager, asks you, "I need to install a new LAN. What should I buy: TCP/IP or Ethernet?" What do you advise?

26. Why do some network managers distribute their servers?

27. Why do some network managers centralize their servers?

28. What are the business benefits of a client/server computing architecture, compared to a mainframe-based architecture?

29. The unit of exchange at the Data Link Layer is the:
    (a) packet
    (b) datagram
    (c) frame
    (d) bit
    (e) byte or octet

30. Applications that NEED a token-passing LAN's deterministic access include:
    (a) industrial processing
    (b) e-mail
    (c) database management
    (d) workstation-to-mainframe
    (e) all of the above

When you have finished this review, go to Appendix A and look at the answer key. Look at any questions you may have missed and understand why you had a different idea. Unless you understand almost all of the technical concepts reviewed here, it would be a good idea for you to read a good basic LAN text, work your way through Mastering Local Area Networks or take a LAN course at your local University Extension before you proceed with this Internetworking training course.

Chapter 1 reviews the Open Systems Interconnection (OSI) Model and then traces the development of internetworking needs. Let's go!

1

The Evolving Need For Internetworking

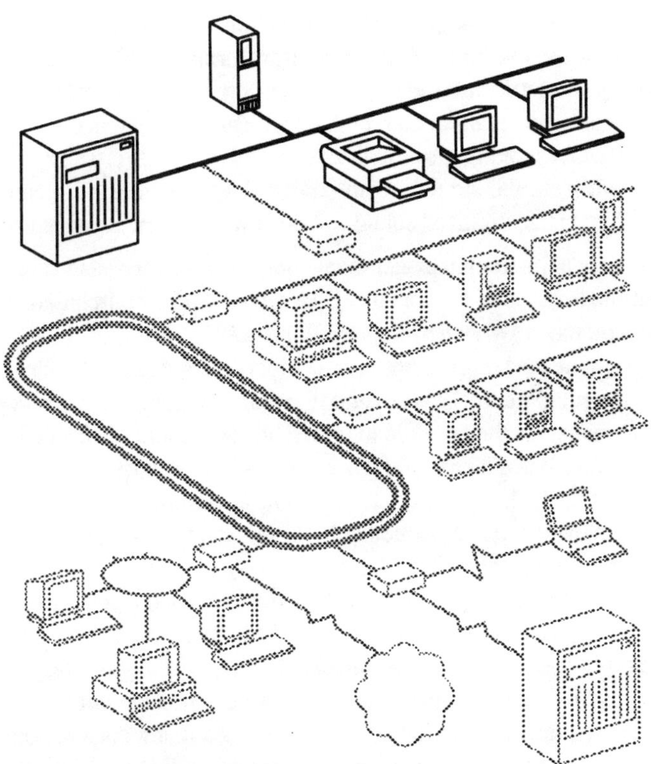

Goals of this Chapter

When you complete this chapter, you will have reviewed:

- ❐ local area network (LAN) concepts
- ❐ the seven layer Open Systems Interconnection (OSI) Model
- ❐ basic internetwork device classifications

You will also complete an inventory of your present network with its infrastructure components, topology and applications.

The First Internetworks

The first LANs were primarily **PC LANs** because they were perceived as a way to allow PCs to share peripherals. In this sense, LANs were initially purchased to save money, not make money. In the second phase of LAN evolution, these PC LANs were transformed into **enterprise LANs**, in which PC LANs, mainframes and minicomputers are integrated into a complete communications infrastructure. The third phase of the evolution will be the transformation of this enterprise LAN into an **information utility** for the corporation: a vital part of the corporate game plan for market share and sales success; in other words, as a tool for making money. As LANs evolved, LAN citizens evolved as well: from the simple PC to powerful workstations with complex color graphics, digitized sound and other high-bandwidth features.

The typical internet manager today must internetwork islands of automation, because of the way that LANs were initially purchased. Many MIS managers watched departmental LANs spring up like weeds throughout the corporation, their components hidden in purchases of "office equipment." This decentralization of purchasing gave department managers the freedom to choose the best solutions for their own workgroup's productivity and accelerated LAN deployment. Unfortunately, this deployment pattern had some disadvantages, which are becoming evident as departmental LANs evolve into components of the corporate information infrastructure. Managers who are trying to bring their departments together are finding divergent and incompatible wiring, interfaces and software as obstacles to integration. In addition to the proliferation of LANs within one building or campus, mergers and the establishment of new offices have accelerated the deployment of wide-area internetworking infrastructures. As many corporations become more globally conscious and more dependent on their offshore sales, network managers find themselves transformed into international network managers.

Before we plunge into a consideration of internet technology and choices, let's spend some time reviewing the **OSI Model's** layers. Refreshing your knowledge of the OSI layers will help you identify where your most urgent problems are – and where to look for a solution.

A Simple LAN

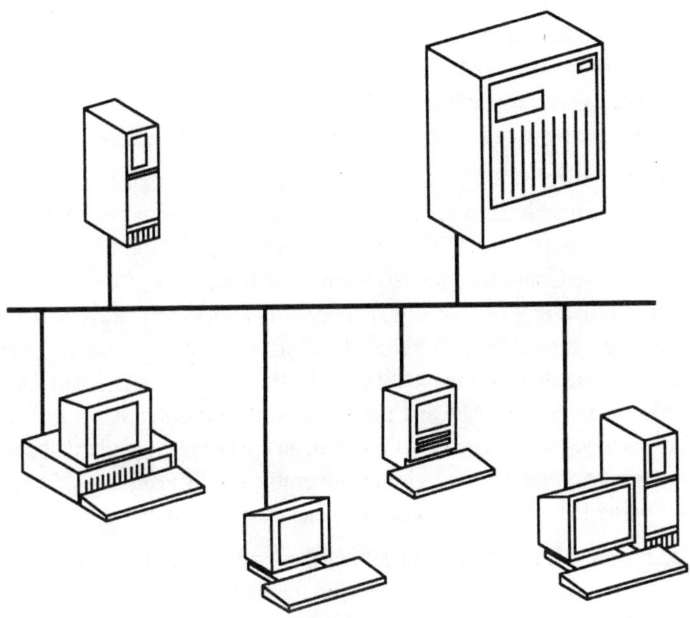

An adaptor card plugs into your network devices and includes software that turns the device's data stream into network-compliant packets. Above the Data Link Layer, all "devices" and functions are exclusively software.

The OSI Model: Reviewing Layers 1 and 2

The Open Systems Interconnection (OSI) Model for network architectures includes specifications for all network functions, from the physical wiring to sophisticated applications support. Each of these functions is encapsulated in a specific layer, which means that you can swap out one implementation of that function (called a **protocol**) and swap in another (at the same layer) whenever your users' needs change and you need new capabilities and functions. Encapsulation means that you can evolve toward future—currently unknown—technologies without having to redesign your entire network architecture.

The OSI Model was originally developed by the International Organization for Standardization (**ISO**), a voluntary international standards organization. In 1984, the OSI Model was approved by the International Consultative Committee for Telephony and Telegraphy (**CCITT**), an official international standards body operating under the United Nations. In the U.S., standards are developed and promoted by the American National Standards Institute (**ANSI**), the Institute for Electrical and Electronics Engineers (**IEEE**) and the National Institute for Standards and Technology (**NIST**). The U.S. Government encourages standards-based product development through the Government OSI Profile (**GOSIP**), a "shopping list" that government agencies must adhere to.

The Physical Layer (Layer 1) defines the hardware and software functions needed to put raw bits onto the medium and transport them to their destination. At the Data Link Layer (Layer 2), bits are recognized as **frames**. This layer divides its functions between the Logical Link Control (LLC) sublayer, which creates a **logical data link** between sender and receiver, and the Media Access Control (MAC) sublayer, which works closely with the Physical Layer. Putting the Physical and MAC functions together creates the well-known IEEE **802**-family LAN standards, of which 802.3 for contention LANs and 802.5 for token-passing rings are the most popular. The LLC sublayer has a common function and a single standard (802.2) to tie all your **access method, medium, topology** and **transmission method** choices together. The IEEE's 802.1 standard provides for network management and bridging.

IEEE Model: Two Layers Only

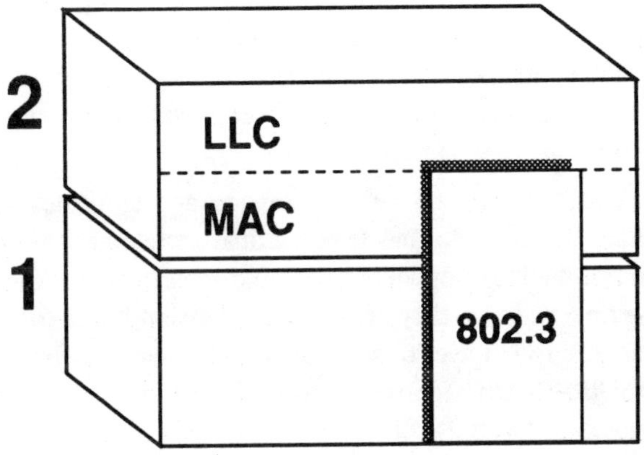

A LAN needs a medium, topology, access method and transmission method. Access methods are CSMA/CD and token-passing. Transmission methods are broadband and baseband.

Medium	The physical data path (the wire)
Topology	How the data path is laid out
Access Method	How the multiple devices share the single data path
Transmission Method	How the devices put their data on the path

Internetwork Devices and the OSI Layers

Network designers have two standard ways of routing packets between sender and receiver at the Network Layer (Layer 3). By analogy with a telephone call, you can set up a **virtual circuit** – a logical connection between sender and receiver – before you send any packets. Alternatively, you can simply send the packets (called **datagram** service) without any preliminary circuit setup. At the Transport Layer (Layer 4) all the failures that occurred at the Network Layer are corrected, including lost or damaged packets. This layer provides quality control of the network's data transport function.

The Session Layer (Layer 5) creates, manages and terminates sessions. Within a session, it creates and deletes virtual circuits and sets up either standard full-duplex or optional half-duplex connections. When LAN users log onto a server, they are making a Session Layer connection. Presentation Layer (Layer 6) services include character code translations (ASCII/EBCDIC, for example) and format translations. The Application Layer (Layer 7) contains only the basic utilities that support the application programs, not the actual applications. File Transfer, Access and Management (FTAM), X.400 message handling and the new network management protocols are the most important Application Layer protocols.

The illustration shows how the common internet device types fit (functionally) into the OSI Model. Chapter 2 focuses on Physical and Data Link Layer internetworking in detail and Chapter 3 focuses on the Network and Applications Layers. Internetworking options in the Session Layer (network operating systems) are covered in *Mastering Advanced Internetworking*.

The OSI Model

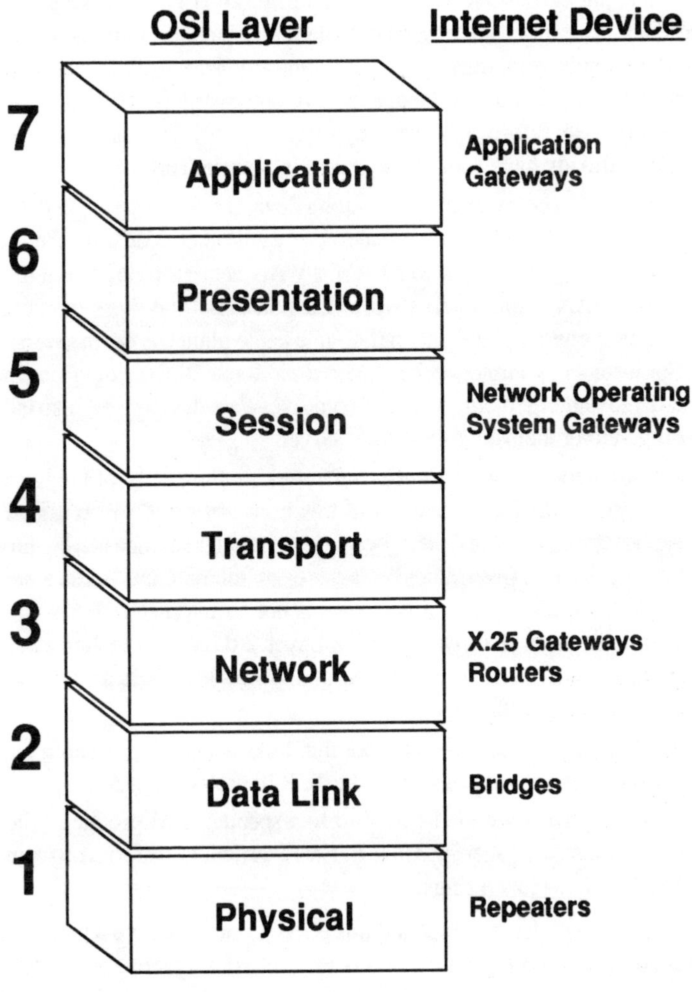

Terminology Notes

The first human attempts at language were almost immediately followed (I am convinced) by the first altercation based on a misunderstanding. The more misunderstandable the particular language is, the more misunderstandings will occur, naturally, and no language is as misunderstandable as the language of internetworking. Before we go any furthur, therefore, let me clarify some terminology issues for readers who already have some background in internetworking:

- A network is composed of computing devices that are connected and potentially able to communicate with each other. You can use the word "network" to refer to a LAN, a WAN, a metropolitan area network (MAN) or an internetwork. Keep in mind that more than one **logical network** can exist on the same cable plant (be **co-resident**). For instance, your network could include some DECnet devices that talk only among themselves and some NetWare devices that also talk only among themselves and their server.
- An internetwork or **internet** is a network that uses any of the internetworking devices discussed in this book (bridges, routers, gateways, packet switches, etc.). In a strict computer science sense, only Layer 3 devices (routers and gateways) are internet devices so a network without routers and gateways is not an internet. A LAN with segments connected by bridges (a Layer 2 device) is technically a **bridged LAN.** Both bridged LANs and **routed internets** are referred to as internets in this book.
- The Internet is a specific internet that links academic, research and commercial networks and uses the TCP/IP protocol stack.
- I use the term Token Ring to refer to a specific IBM product; other companies sell token-passing network products, referred to here generically as token rings.

By the time you have completed this course, you will have a thorough grounding in the correct use of many internetworking terms and will be well able to navigate the confusing shoals of vendor marketing.

Let's move on now to the first two Layers and their specific device types – repeaters and bridges.

Project – Chapter 1

Before we plunge into a consideration of internet options, take some time to prepare an inventory of your current network:

- ❐ Devices
    - Total number of devices attached to the LAN or internet
    - Specific number attached to each segment
    - Total number and distribution by segment of high-performance workstations, desktop video stations and other "bandwidth hogs"
    - percent of the whole that these workstations represent
- ❐ Servers
    - Server numbers and locations
    - % load on each server
- ❐ Current Infrastructure (bridges, routers, gateways)
    - Placement of current internet infrastructure devices
    - Detailed topology map
- ❐ Traffic
    - Daily traffic load in the local networks
    - Internet traffic load (11% is average; could be 25% or more)
    - Pattern (uniform or bursty)
- ❐ Applications (types)
    - delay-sensitive
    - requiring reliability
    - core business
    - key productivity tools (e-mail; whatever the end users depend on most)

These questions provide you with a framework for analyzing your network. Projects, questions and exercises following each chapter will ask you to apply the information contained in the chapter to your own network. Refer back to this inventory as you work through these exercises.

Key Words

The words and phrases highlighted in **bold**, also listed below, represent key concepts in this chapter. Since this chapter is a review, most of these terms are well-known to you. If there are any terms that are not familiar to you, take the time now to review their definition based on the training text.

PC LANs
enterprise LANs
information utility
OSI Model
protocol
ISO
CCITT
ANSI
IEEE
NIST
GOSIP
frames
logical data link
802
access method
medium
topology
transmission method
virtual circuit
datagram
logical network
co-resident
internet
bridged LAN
routed internet

2

Repeaters and Bridges

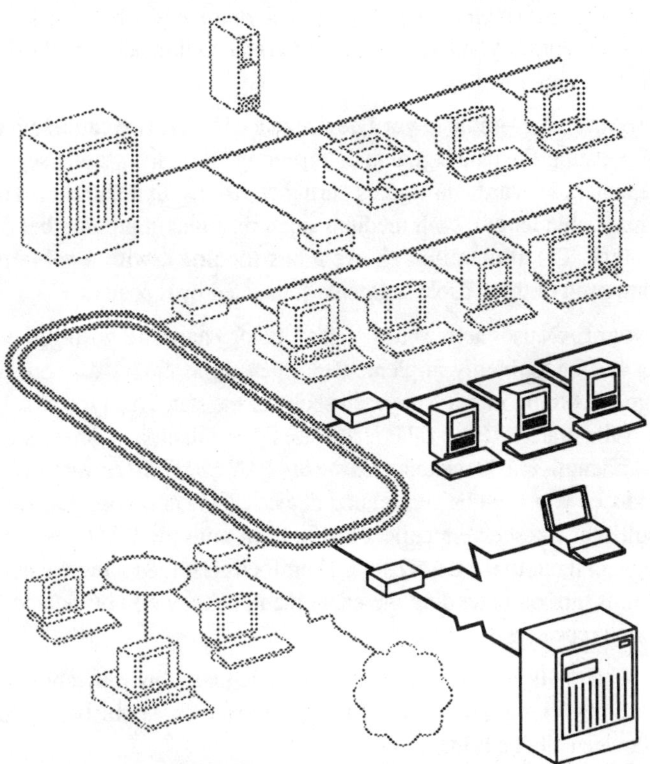

Goals of This Chapter

This chapter focuses on repeaters and bridges. By the end of this chapter you should be able to:

- ❐ Understand repeaters and their place in the network
- ❐ Describe how to fit a bridge into the OSI Model's hierarchy of functions
- ❐ Be able to describe how both Spanning Tree and Source Route Bridging work and what the advantages of each are
- ❐ Succinctly list the major business benefits and disadvantages of bridges

Repeaters

All cable types have maximum lengths because all media gradually weaken the data signals until they are indistinguishable from "noise" signals. A single Ethernet thick cable segment, for example, cannot be more than 500 meters long. If you want your LAN cable to extend beyond that limit, you have to use a **repeater** to link additional cable to your existing plant.

A repeater is a simple Layer 1 device that connects two cable segments by boosting the data signal and "repeating" it on the second segment. Repeaters forward jam signals during collisions. In addition to a maximum cable length, each medium supports a maximum number of repeaters. The illustration shows a bus topology, with a cable plant composed of three cable segments connected by repeaters

If your LAN uses active hubs, a star topology and UTP wiring, the vendor has undoubtedly implemented repeaters in the hubs to boost the signals coming into it from each spoke of the star. This type of LAN is also illustrated. If the UTP is 10BaseT-compliant, a segment's maximum length is 100 meters. (*Mastering LAN Enabling Technologies* introduces you to hubs and related devices. Concentrators, fanouts and multiport transceivers collect traffic from multiple LAN devices and connect them to the LAN cable. Their focus is on reducing the number of taps, not on extending the cable plant, so they do not include integrated repeaters.)

Repeaters allow you to extend your cable plant, but they are not true internetworking devices. Let's move on to a more sophisticated Layer 2 device called a bridge.

Bus Wiring

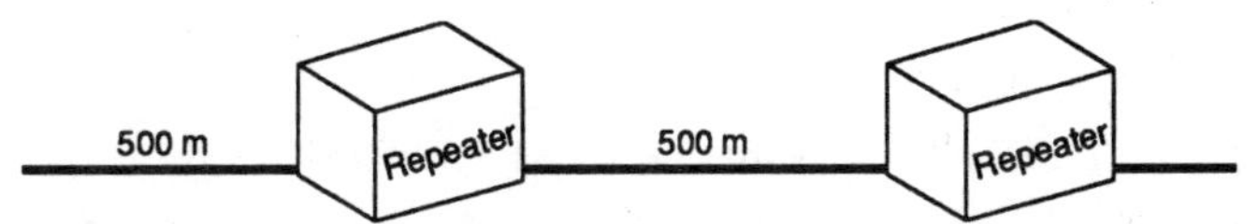

Hub/UTP Installations

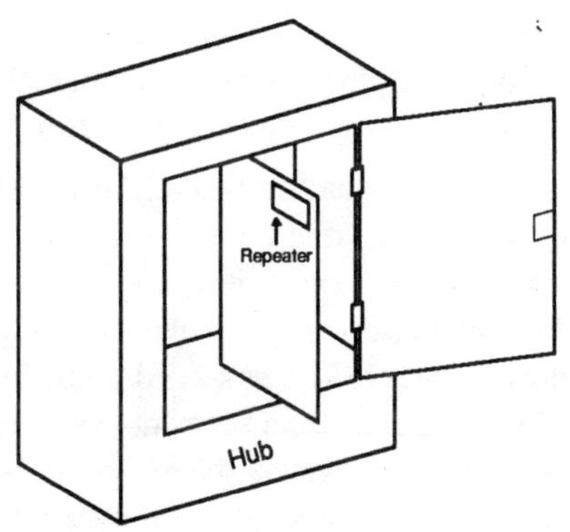

Filter or Forward?

Let's review the format of a typical Data Link frame before we move on to bridging specifics. Layer 1 software creates the **Preamble**, 8 bytes that say "I'm a frame." At Layer 2, the sender adds four fields:

- a **Destination Address**
- a **Source Address**
- a **Field Type**, which specifies the Layer 3 protocol, if any.
- a **Frame Check Sequence** (FCS), which is a cyclical redundancy check (CRC). The CRC allows the receiver to detect the presence of bit errors.

A bridge processes Data Link Layer frames, either passing them or not passing them between segments of a LAN, based on an analysis of the two addresses. The Field Type allows the Layer 2 device to know what kind of Layer 3 protocol the packet contains; it does not include full Layer 3 protocol information. We will revisit the Field Type later in this chapter, when we discuss filtering.

Let's start with a bridge that links two LAN segments. (Remember, as soon as you put a bridge between two LANs, they are no longer separate LANs, just **segments** of the same LAN.) Each segment is connected to the bridge by an **interface cable**; the bridge has a LAN **interface card** for every physical connection it makes. (See A Learning Bridge's Dynamic Address Table on page 25.)

The bridge reads the source and destination Data Link addresses of every frame that comes to it from the two segments. Based on the addresses, it decides what to do with the frame, a decision process called **filtering**. If the two addresses are on the same segment, the bridge **drops** the frame. Bridges reduce unneeded traffic by dropping frames that don't need to proliferate from segment to segment. If the destination address is on another segment the bridge is also connected to, it passes the frame on, a process called **forwarding**. But how does a bridge know where the various addresses are?

Bridge Filtering

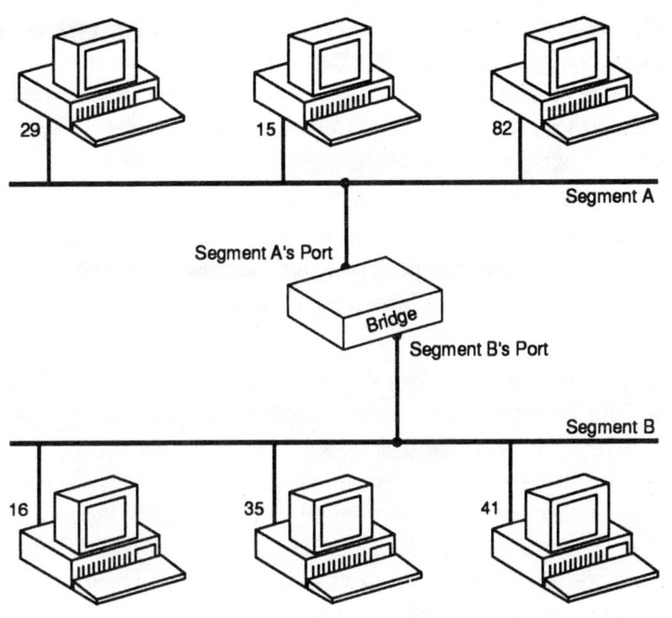

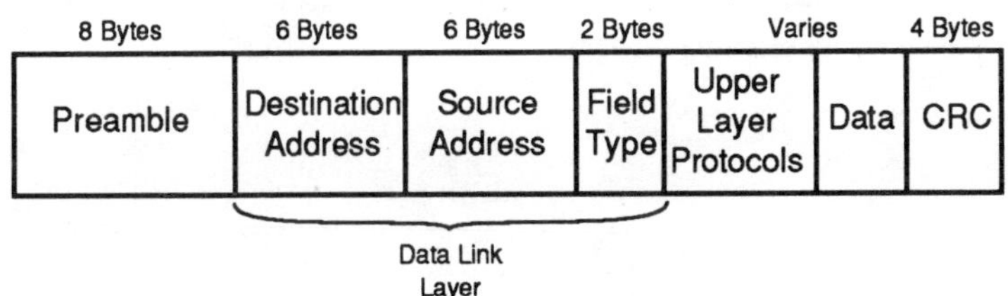

A Frame Format

Learning Bridges

A **learning bridge** learns what segment the various addresses are on by reading the source addresses of all the frames that travel on the LAN. The bridge uses these addresses to create a **bridging address table** in memory, listing the addresses and what segments they are on. The bridge consults its table when deciding whether to drop or forward a frame. (Most literature refers to this as "filter or forward.") If the address does not exist in the table, the bridge will forward it.

A learning bridge begins creating its table as soon as it is turned on. Until the table is well under way, the bridge spends most of its time forwarding. The table-building process proceeds dynamically until the bridge is turned off. New information always overwrites older information.

If an address hasn't been heard from in a specified period of time (it hasn't appeared as a source address, in other words), the bridge deletes it from the table. This **aging** process deletes entries that are so old they may be wrong. For instance, you might have moved a PC from one office to another and it may now be on a different LAN segment. The bridge's aging algorithm (design) can be summarized as: It's better to assume you don't know and listen for new information than to assume you do know when you probably don't.

The first generation of bridges built tables statically, through an operator's manual intervention. This is still a reasonable option for LANs with ten or fewer devices. Most bridges sold today service much larger LANs and are learning bridges.

Connecting a Local Segment to a Backbone

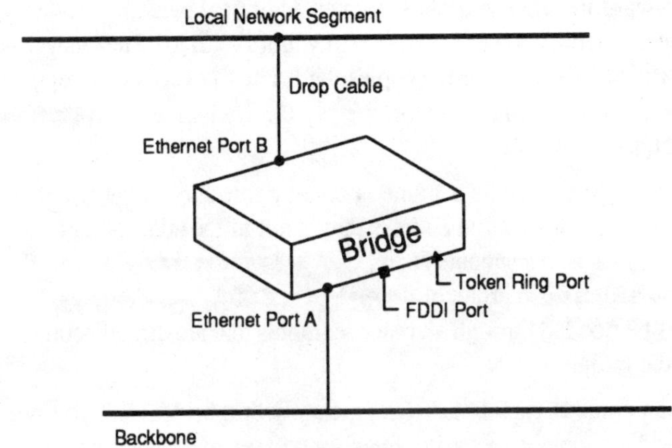

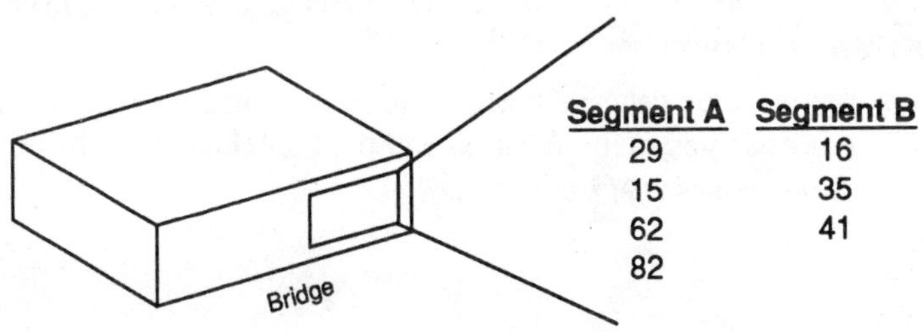

Segment A	Segment B
29	16
15	35
62	41
82	

A Learning Bridge's Dynamic Address Table

Flooding

Bridges don't have to just connect two LAN segments. In our illustration, segments A, B and C are all directly connected. The same filtering and forwarding process applies, with an additional twist: If you decide to forward, which "other" segment do you forward to? The answer is: all of them! When the bridge copies the frame to every other segment except the originating segment, we say the frame has been **flooded** through the network.

In this example, assume a frame is coming into the bridge from segment A with a destination address that is not in the address table. The bridge floods it to segments B and C. A **broadcast frame**, whose destination address is a protocol-dependent code for "all addresses," will always be flooded through all other segments that are directly connected to the bridge.

You can connect remote LAN segments with a bridge, but you need two bridges, one at each site. Remote bridges are sometimes called **half-bridges**, because only half the processing occurs in each half of the connection. Each remote bridge reads the frames that come down its wire(s) and then sends the frame out on one of its wide-area ports. (We'll discuss wide-area transport options in detail in Chapter 4.) A remote bridge can connect to two or more LAN segments at each site, just as a local bridge can.

Be aware of traffic patterns, however. Remember that a bridge has a finite processing capacity. What do you think a bridge does if it receives more frames than it can handle?

Flooding

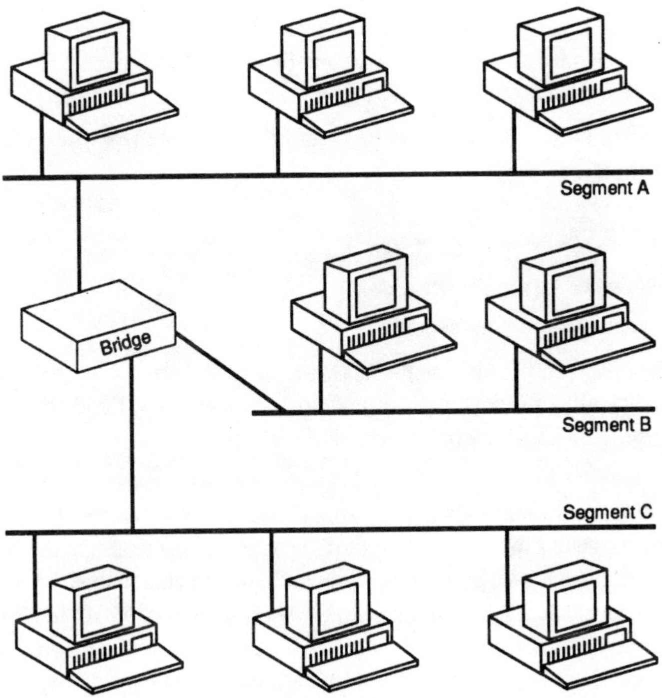

Complex Filtering

Unfortunately, bridges have no interactive flow control capability, so a bridge that gets overloaded will **choke** and start to drop incoming frames. This weakness stems from their status as Data Link Layer (Layer 2) devices: their expertise is limited to the drop or forward decision. Bridges do not communicate with end user devices, they simply respond to the frames that are present on the LAN. Of course, it is precisely this lack of complexity that makes the bridge very fast.

In addition to addresses, bridges can filter on other Data Link Layer information:

- frame size
- frame type (broadcast, for example)
- Network Layer protocol
- what else can you think of?

The bridge can "filter" on the Network Layer (Layer 3) protocol, without actually "processing" the protocol, because of the Field Type part of the Data Link control information.

Bridges connect two segments that may contain different media, topologies, access methods and transmission methods, but use the same LLC or Data Link protocol. Return to Chapter 1 and examine the IEEE Model once more. You can see that the four elements that a bridge can connect easily are all contained in the combination of MAC and Physical Layer specifications. Because two MAC sublayers are communicating, these are also known as **MAC bridges**. With considerably more engineering effort, you can connect an 802.3 (Ethernet-like) LAN to an 802.5 LAN, using what is variously known as a 3-to-5, .3/.5 or **Dot3-to-Dot5 bridge**, a specific type of MAC bridge. Why do you think these bridges are so much more difficult to engineer than Ethernet–Ethernet bridges?

Remote Bridging

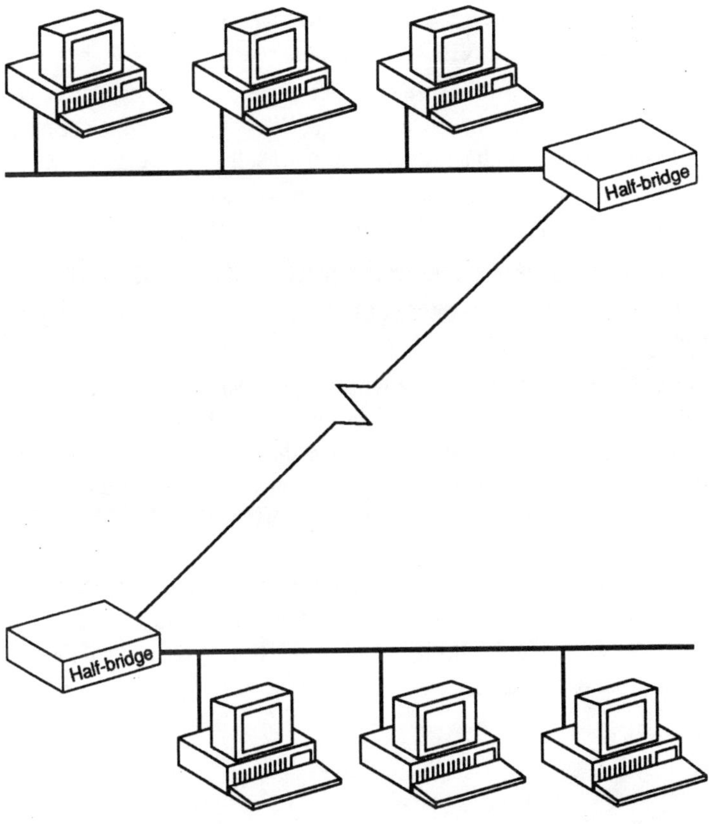

Thou Shalt Not Loop

If you value reliability, you might want to use two bridges to link the same segments. The two bridges could share the load and they would not need flow control, right? Well, not quite. If you allow more than one path to exist between sender and receiver in a bridged LAN, you have a loop and this is VERY bad because

- The same frame will be seen by both bridges and, if forwardable, will be forwarded. This means the receiver will get two or more copies of the same frame, with usually disastrous results. But it gets worse.
- Data Link frames circulate forever, since they have no lifetime control. So the frame will be forwarded and copied again and again.

So you must never allow loops in your bridged LAN. Every segment must have one and only one active path between it and every other segment. This can be a challenge in LANs with complex topologies.

Loop discovery software can help you prevent loops. Bridges send out loop discovery frames at regular intervals and see if they reappear. If they do, a loop has been created and the bridge that discovers this shuts itself down to break the loop. You can also use this capability to increase LAN reliability by putting in "hot standby" bridges. The standby sends out periodic loop discovery frames and as long as the frames keep looping back the standby remains inactive. If two or more frames fail to return to their sender, the standby is justified in deciding that one of the regular bridges has failed. It then turns itself on and starts processing frames.

A Network Loop

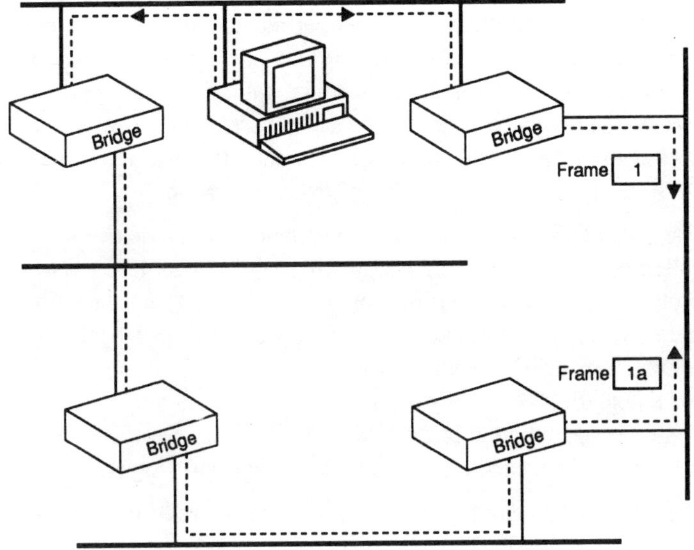

Bridging Standards

The IEEE adopted the **Spanning Tree** (802.1, section D) standard for creating healthy topologies in 802.3 and 802.4 (token bus) LANs. Spanning Tree-compliant bridges preclude loops and speed **convergence** on a best path by creating a rooted branching tree structure. With the simple illustration shown opposite, the tree structure, where one bridge acts as the root, isn't very obvious. However, in complex bridged LANs, where multiple potential paths exist, the speedy discovery of a fastest-path through a maze of possibilities is an extremely important attribute. The Spanning Tree algorithm was developed by Dr. Radia Perlman of Digital Equipment Corporation.

The 802.5 token ring subcommittee embraced an alternative scheme, called **source route bridging**, in which the source device, not the bridge, ensures that loops do not occur, by specifying the path the frame is allowed to traverse. The source specifies the path by listing the addresses of the bridges the frame must visit on its journey. Can you see a potential flaw in this mechanism? (If you are familiar with the Source Route option in TCP/IP, this is NOT the same software. Source route bridging occurs at the Data Link, not Network, Layer.)

The 802.5 subcommittee also developed the **Source Routing-Transparent Bridging** (SR-TB) specification that provides Spanning Tree on the Ethernet side, source route bridging on the token side and an algorithm to transform the divergent frame formats and loop-prevention mechanisms. (We will revisit many of these issues in more detail in *Mastering Advanced Internetworking*.)

Loop Discovery

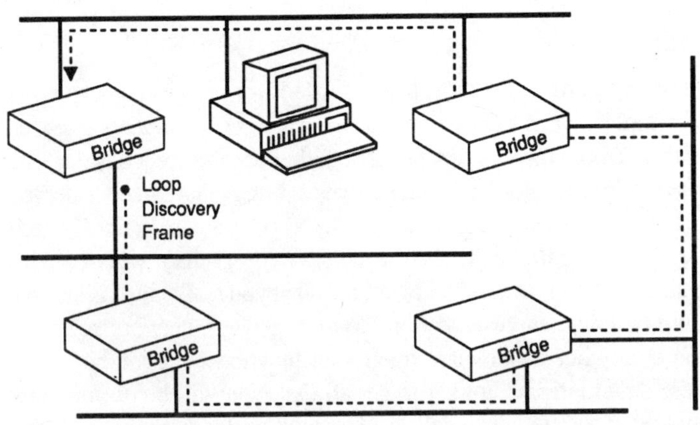

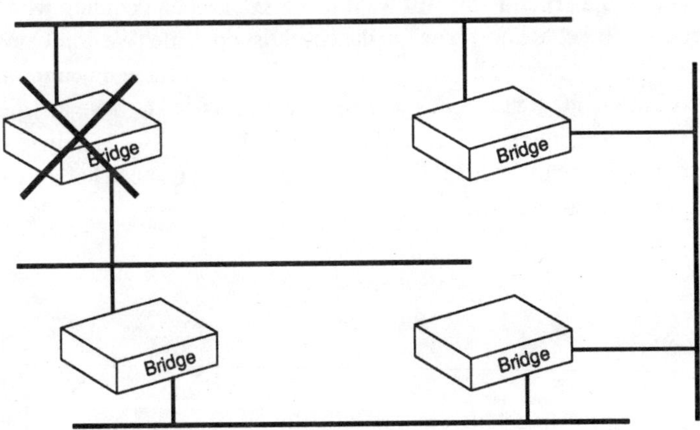

Bridges periodically send out loop discovery frames. If a bridge gets its frame back, a loop exists and it will shut itself down to break the loop.

Choosing the Right Bridge

- **Smart bridge**
- Intelligent bridge
- Brouter

These are some of the most popular names for bridges that can do the very sophisticated filtering we discussed under *Complex Filtering*, can take on simple Layer 3 functions, or both. For instance, consider least-cost routing. Wouldn't it be nice to have a bridge that can consider traffic levels on its wide-area network (WAN) ports and selectively choose the cheapest path or the fastest path (as you prefer), whenever it is available? Sure, it would. However, if what you really need is alternate route-building, sophisticated traffic management, network segmentation or any one of the other true router functions and you buy one of these "alternatives" hoping to get all that, you will be disappointed. These devices are what I call "bridges with a college education." They are not router substitutes.

Some of the criteria you will want to consider when deciding which bridge to purchase are shown in the checklist opposite. We don't have space here to cover all the possible questions in sufficient detail, but you can see the trend. Focus on what your users need to have in order to make the company successful in its marketplace. Price is only relevant in relation to value received. Figure out what you need before you start talking to vendors.

A Buyer Checklist

What applications will be running on the various sections of the LAN?

- ❒ High-bandwidth?
- ❒ Is your traffic bursty?
- ❒ How much internet traffic are you likely to have? With simple office applications, about 15% of the available traffic will need to be forwarded.
- ❒ Are you carrying core business applications? You need reliability. Try "hot standbys."

What are your security needs?

- ❒ Do you intend to segregate users according to their higher-level protocols?
- ❒ Their packet types? This will dictate the complexity of the filtering capability you should buy.

What are your server needs?

- ❒ Where are your servers placed? Don't put a bridge between users and their servers. Find out what services the users are actually logging on to, not just what they're supposed to be limited to.

What are your projected needs?

- ❒ If your user needs are burgeoning, are you likely to need a routed internet in 3 to 5 years? Make today's purchases with tomorrow's, as well as today's, needs in mind.
- ❒ Is your industry undergoing consolidation? Many WAN internets are the result of mergers and acquisitions.
- ❒ Is your overseas presence increasing? Investigate CCITT standards-based products.

Bridges: Pro and Con

Bridges have many benefits:

- They're fast.
- They're cheap.
- They are not higher-layer protocol-specific. An Ethernet bridge can forward DECnet, IP, IPX or other packet types transparently.
- Smart ones are able to filter on many criteria.

Bridge disadvantages cluster in two areas:

- There is no segmentation. Broadcast storms and other problems proliferate at will throughout the LAN and there is little security in the infrastructure itself. Remember that bridges create one single LAN, with a single address and naming space.
- There is no flow control. Bridges can only respond to the traffic as presented. They cannot dialog with end user devices – requesting "bandwidth hogs" to slow down, for example – or each other.

There are many networks for which bridges are the best connection solution. When you have read more about routers, you will be in a better position to decide whether your network should bypass routing and focus exclusively on bridging. In the next chapter, you will meet routers and gateways, two important upper-layer internetworking devices.

A Bridged LAN Creates A Single Address and Name Space

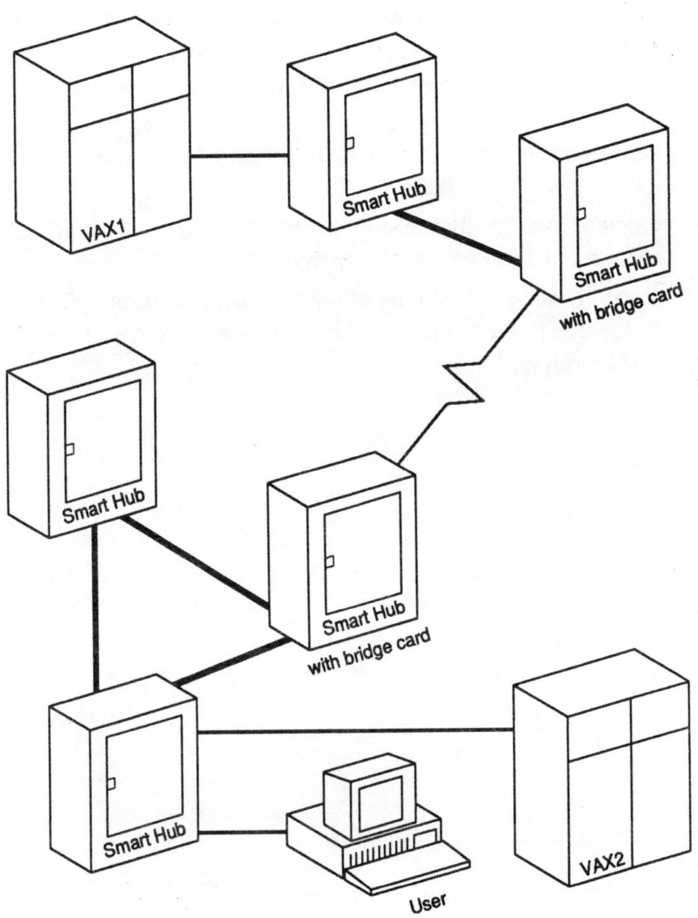

Summary

- Repeaters link identical cable types, extending the length of a cable plant.
- Bridges process Data Link frames, linking separate LANs into a single LAN. They are blind to upper-layer protocols (except as filtering criteria) and focus primarily on source and destination Data Link addresses. Bridges can drop, forward or flood frames as needed.
- Bridges are fast and relatively inexpensive and smart ones can perform very complex filtering.
- Learning bridges dynamically create an address table, adding, changing and aging entries as appropriate.
- To prevent loops, most bridges follow either the Spanning Tree or the Source Route Bridging standard. A loop can cause chaos and LAN paralysis.

Review – Chapter 2

1. Why do designers incorporate repeaters in hubs?
2. The components of a typical frame include the Preamble, ________, ________, ________, ________, ___________.
3. Does a strictly Layer 2 device know what Layer 3 protocol the packet contains? If so, how?
4. The process by which a bridge decides how to handle a frame is called ________.
5. If a bridge decides to throw a frame out, we say the frame was _________.
6. A _________ bridge creates a dynamic address table based on __________ addresses.
7. If a bridge has no entry for a specific address in its table, it will _______ it if it is attached to only 2 segments and _____ it if it is connected to more than 2.
8. What problem was the Spanning Tree standard developed to solve? How does it work?
9. In source route bridging, it is the ________ that calculates the path to the destination end user, while in a Spanning Tree network, the ________ does this work.
10. List at least 4 ways you could use a smart bridge to filter and isolate your LAN traffic. What two types of filtering will be most important in your network?
11. Bridges cannot communicate with each other or with end users on traffic management issues; that is a router function. Does the existence of loop discovery frames contradict this? Why or why not?
12. The three most important benefits of bridges, for your network, are ________, ___________, and ___________.

Key Words

The words and phrases highlighted in **bold** represent key concepts in this chapter. Please take the time now to write down your own definitions of these terms, using the list below, or use additional paper if needed. Then compare your efforts to the training text. This is an excellent way for you to determine weak points in the breadth and depth of your understanding of this chapter.

repeater
Preamble
Destination Address
Source Address
Field Type
Frame Check Sequence
segments
interface cable
interface card
filtering
drops
forwarding
learning bridge
bridging address table
aging
flooded
broadcast frame
half-bridge
choke
MAC bridges
Dot3-to-Dot3 bridge
Loop Discovery
Spanning Tree
convergence
source route bridging
Source Routing-Transparent Bridging
Smart Bridge

3

Routers and Gateways

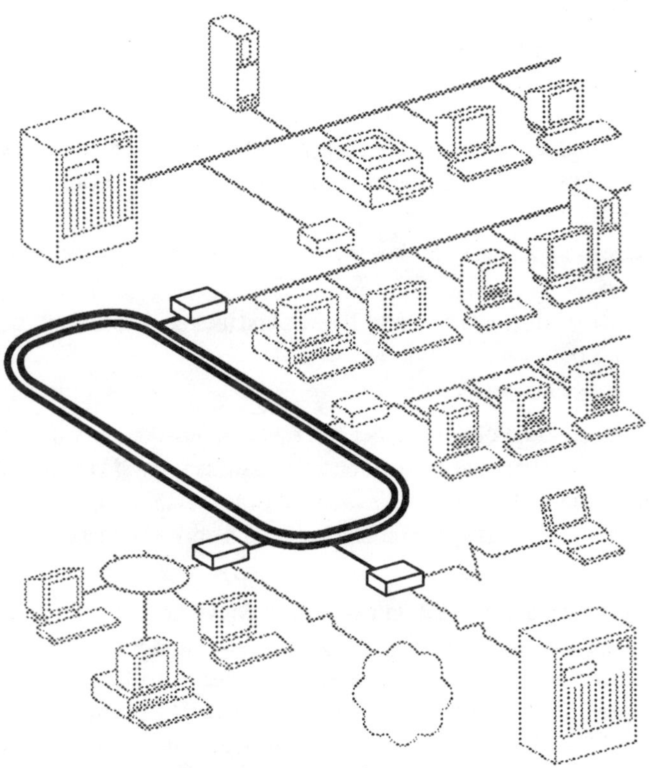

Goals of this Chapter

- ❒ Describe the difference between bridges and routers, routers and gateways, routed internets and bridged LANs, and routed internets and hybrid internets
- ❒ Choose the best internet device mix for your network
- ❒ Make thoughtful predictions about the future of router and gateway platforms and understand how this will affect your business options.

Many of the topics in this chapter are continued in more detail in *Mastering Advanced Internetworking*.

How Routers Work

Bridges can't solve every internetworking need. Specifically, they cannot

- Build multiple alternate routes.
- Manage traffic loads.
- Segment/partition/set up firewalls.

These capabilities are beyond what is possible at the Data Link Layer, so we need to move on to Network Layer (Layer 3) functions and a device called the **router**. Functioning at the "internet layer," these devices create a true internet infrastructure, with exciting functional implications. A router

- Doesn't read every packet that comes down the wire, like a bridge does.
- Can communicate dynamically with end user devices and other routers. Routers are active in the network.
- Is protocol-specific.

The first section of this chapter will focus on how routers work. In the second we will move on to the business issues involved in routed internets and in the last we'll see how to integrate routers with other internet devices. Let's start by examining how end users and routers communicate.

An end user system (**ES**, in OSI terminology) can only communicate with a router by addressing it directly. When a user device wants to make a connection to another device in another LAN (known as **going off-net**), it must ask a router to create the internet (network-to-network) connection. The ES's network software creates the packet with the local router's address in the Data Link Layer address fields and the ultimate destination in the Network Layer fields. Only the router, as a Network Layer device or Intermediate System (**IS**), reads or cares about the ultimate destination. Other devices in the network merely note the immediate destination of the packet. (Remember as you proceed through this chapter that a "device" is an entity that performs the indicated function, so it can be entirely software.)

A Generic Packet – Layer 3

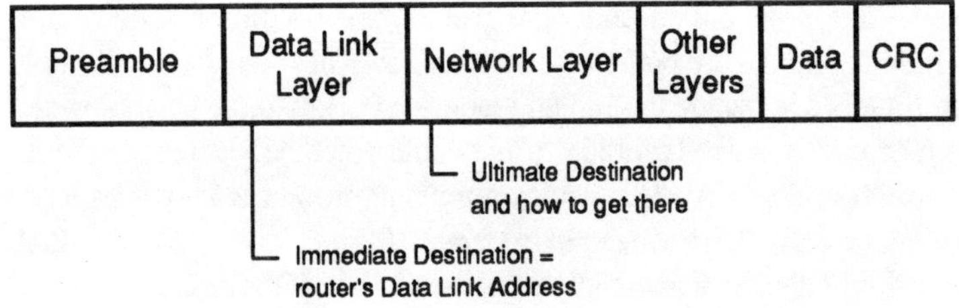

Data Link and Network Layers include addresses and control information. Specifics vary widely with protocol type.

Basic Route-Building

When a router receives a packet destined for another network, it must create a route or path to the foreign network. A route is really just a list of router-to-router **hops**. Routers move packets through the internet by passing them on to each other. With every hand-off, the router rewrites the Data Link addressing so the next destination is the next router on the path.

Now, each router makes its own independent estimation of what the best path is. Routers learn, for instance, how congested individual wide-area links are and how congested their **neighbor routers** are. These neighbors are potential candidates for "next destination" status, so routers can decide to send an incoming packet to the least crowded router among several candidates that could potentially get the packet to where it needs to go. This decision-making process is known as load-balancing, which we visited in extremely limited form in Chapter 2. A router will decide dynamically what the address of the next hop will be, based on a **cost** calculation. A more expensive option could cost more in dollars (on WAN links), in time (slower-speed WAN links, lower bandwidth LANs, congested routers), in number of hops to the destination, or in other factors.

In the illustration, you can see that routers provide **redundant paths** if a router fails. If Router 3 fails or becomes significantly impaired, Router 1 can still build routes to Network G via Router 5 plus Router 4. This route "costs" 2 hops, compared to 1 hop via Router 3, but if the lowest cost route disappears, your local router can still build **alternate routes**. (Did you notice that the bridge is not included in the route calculation? It is a lower-layer detail, irrelevant to a router.) This is one part of how a router delivers high reliability to an internet.

Route Building

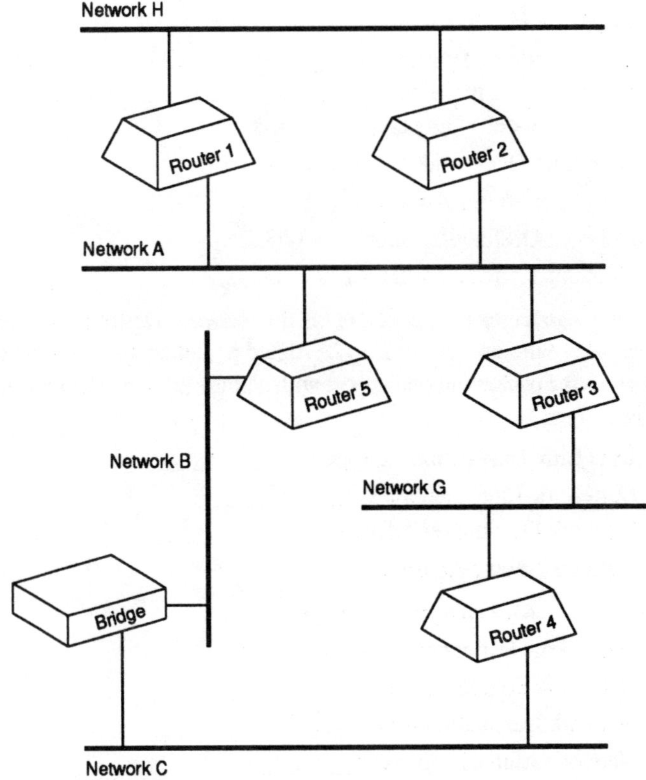

Let's Practice: Router Addressing

In the following exercise, we will use **dotted decimal notation** in which a network number and a local address are separated by a dot. So address 123 on network 51 is known as 51.123.

ES 129.01 wants to communicate with ES 37.382, so it sends a packet to its local router, Router 1, whose address is 105. (In a real internet, you would have more than one router connecting segments; this is a simplified model.) Let's create the packet:

Data Link Destination Address = 105

Data Link Source Address = 101

Network Destination Address = 37.382

Network Source Address = 129.101

Router 1 receives the packet, reads the Network Destination Address, sees where the packet needs to be routed to and creates the best route. It sends the packet out on the port with address 30.269. The packet now has:

Data Link Destination Address ______________

Data Link Source Address ________________

Network Destination Address _______________

Network Source Address ____________

The packet that leaves Router 2 has:

Data Link Destination Address ______________

Data Link Source Address ________________

Network Destination Address _______________

Network Source Address ____________

The packet that leaves Router 3 has:

Data Link Destination Address ______________

Data Link Source Address ________________

Network Destination Address _______________

Network Source Address ____________

The answers are located in Appendix A. How did you do? Don't move on until this concept is entirely clear to you.

Router Addressing

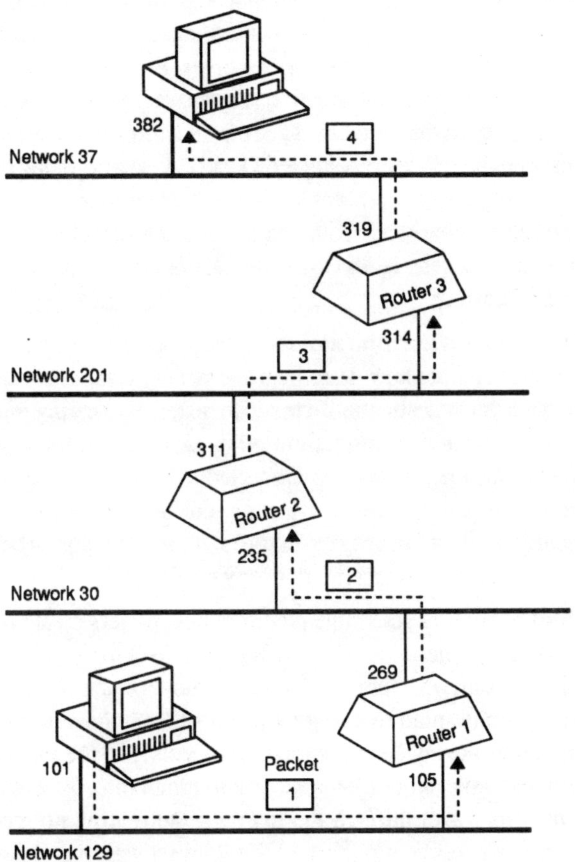

The Power of Advertising – Internet-style

How do end users know where their local routers are (where = the Data Link address)? In most architectures, routers and users **advertise** their existence to each other. One popular way of doing this has routers broadcasting packets on the networks they are directly connected to (using the HELLO protocol, for example). End users read the advertisements and note the information. The exact content of the advertisement varies with the protocol. The routers learn the addresses of local end users indirectly by reading the Data Link source address of all the packets that pass by, a process known as **backward learning.** The second popular scenario has both end users and routers broadcasting advertisement packets. In an OSI-style network, this is known as **ES/IS address flooding.**

End user systems learn the address of an immediate destination to send their packets to, but how do routers learn enough about the network to know what "next destination" choice to make? By sharing information with each other and creating **routing tables**, routers learn how to get to networks they are not directly connected to and use their tables to calculate the lowest cost route. By communicating with each other dynamically, routers always have up-to-date information. These tables are also referred to as logical **topology maps.**

Routing protocols determine precisely how routers create routing tables: how they determine costs, what kind of incoming update information they accept, what they send out in their own update broadcasts, and so on. (Keep in mind that routing protocols only govern how routers interact; they are not Network Layer protocols, like the Internet Protocol. For example, an IP router needs a routing protocol. IP determines how packets travel through the internet; the routing protocol determines how routers communicate.) We'll investigate one of the earliest, simplest routing protocols in detail next.

Routers Advertise

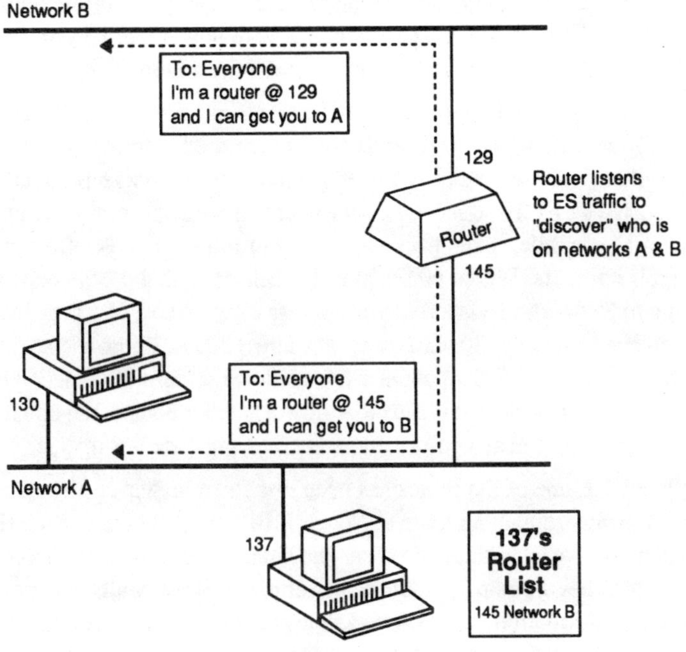

RIP In Detail

The Routing Information Protocol (**RIP**) is being replaced by other protocols in complex internets, primarily because the element it uses to make its calculation (its **metric**) is a simple **hop count**. The HELLO protocol uses an equally simple metric, a time delay in milliseconds. RIP's simplicity makes it a perfect example of how a routing protocol works, so we will use it as we practice building a routing table.

Let's step inside an IP router using RIP as it is first turned on and begins to build its routing table. It sends out a **routing update** composed of everything it knows, which is who it is and which networks it is directly connected to. Every 60 seconds, our router will send out continuing updates. Meanwhile, it sits back and listens to routing updates from its neighbor routers. Within 60 seconds, it has learned that it can create a route to Network 11 via a router at address 225 at a cost of 1 hop, that it can reach Network 30 via a router at address 329 in 1 hop, and so on. When the routing update counter counts down to zero at 60 seconds and our router decides it is time to send out another update, the update will include all the new information received since the last update.

In Round 3, one of the routes has been lost and a higher-cost route is now the only remaining route to Network 10. You will notice that RIP routers believe everything they hear and immediately pass it on; in other words, they **gossip**. Two of the newer protocols only allow routers to share information about networks they are directly attached to. RIP has some limitations that we won't discuss here, but in general a routing protocol creates routing tables complex enough to allow a router to find any network in the internet, no matter how distant. It is sometimes said that routers know the entire internet structure, that their topology maps are all-inclusive. While this isn't strictly true of all routers at all times, it is true that a router knows enough about the entire internet to be able to get a packet to any other network, and that's all that matters to the end users.

Now that we have an understanding of how routers work, let's discuss the business benefits and costs of using a routed internet.

A Routing Table

Round 2

Network	Address of Router	Hop Count
10	411	2
11	225	1
30	329	1

Round 3: Two new routers are added

Network	Address of Router	Hop Count
10	366	1
10	411	2
11	225	1
30	329	1
30	544	2

Round 4: A route is lost; a slower option gets first place

Network	Address of Router	Hop Count
10	411	2
11	225	1
30	329	1
30	544	2

A routing table usually lists destinations in descending numerical order for quick lookup. They usually list the quickest route first – lowest hop count in this case.

A Business View of Routing

- Routers deliver reliability for your internet. Alternate paths protect the infrastructure when one element fails.
- Routers partition cleanly. Problems remain local.
- Routers are smarter and therefore more manageable and programmable. Filtering and security options are very complex.
- Routers manage traffic to give you congestion control and load balancing throughout the internet.

Many of these benefits are a direct result of routers being active in the network, constantly talking to each other or to end users.

Choose routers for your internet if it is your mission to support:

- applications that CANNOT fail, because they represent the company's core business.
- traffic-intensive applications or devices (so-called bandwidth hogs) that are likely to periodically shut out bridges, impacting performance for other applications and users.
- applications that will create high levels of LAN–LAN traffic.

You need a routed internet if you need strong segmentation or you must support mission-critical applications.

A routed internet will also deliver some potential negatives:

- In the near term, you should buy all your routers from the same company. Every vendor's version of Layer 3 software is subtly different from every other vendor's.
- Routers are a bit slower and more expensive than bridges. More functionality means more processing and more cost.
- Routers require you to be more technically educated, to deal with more complex issues, to make more protocol choices and to educate your staff accordingly.

Core Business

This project will help you to research, understand and focus on your company's core business. When you know what your company's core business is, you can develop a plan to ensure that the applications that support core business activities get top priority for network resources.

- ❐ What is your mission within the corporation?
  To deliver ________________ to ________________

- ❐ What is your company's core business?

- ❐ What applications support this core business?
  All business activities support the corporate goal of increasing profits, but only some applications support the core business you listed above. Focus on these applications first when allocating your network resources.
  - ❐ Order entry?
  - ❐ Parts delivery?
  - ❐ Immediate line stock/bond reports?
  - ❐ Manufacturing plant?
  - ❐ Daily production summary?
  - ❐ Traffic reports?
  - ❐ ____________________
  - ❐ ____________________

Hybrid Internets

You don't have to choose only bridges or only routers for your internet. An internet that uses both bridges and routers is called a **hybrid internet**. One kind of hybrid internet is shown in the illustration opposite, with some segments part of a single **bridged LAN** and other segments part of a **routed internet**. In this illustration we are showing standalone devices.

You decide to create a hybrid internet when some segments of the internet need high reliability and other router benefits while other segments, with mostly local traffic, unroutable protocols, low-bandwidth user devices or a combination, should be part of a bridged LAN. In the illustration, the upper building constitutes a single bridged LAN; the second building has both routers and bridges. The first building is labeled Network 5667 because this bridged LAN, although composed of different access methods, topologies and (probably) media, is a single network. In the second building, Network 4590 is separated from the backbone by a bridge, while the other two labeled networks use routers to connect to the backbone. What is the unknown network's number? (The answer is in Appendix A.) Can you explain why? Do you understand all the implications of its being in the same address space as one of the other networks? Remember that routers can only "see" other routers, while everything else (that operates at a lower Layer) is an end user to them.

A more initially expensive option that can give you very cost-effective migration paths is a hardware platform with bridging and routing options in board-level products or software. A platform with only bridging is a bridge. Add an IP routing board or software and you have an IP router in the same box. If this **integrated bridge/router** receives a packet type it doesn't recognize, it simply bridges the packet. For instance, an integrated bridge/router can route DECnet packets but would have to bridge DEC's LAT (local area transport) traffic. (Some protocols, like LAT, are **unroutable protocols**, because they are too time-sensitive, must take specific routes or for other reasons.) Without the bridging option, LAT users would be restricted to local communication; without the routing option, the DECnet users would have an inherently less reliable and secure internet. A brouter or smart bridge (see Chapter 2) is NOT an integrated bridge/router.

Hybrid Internet Case

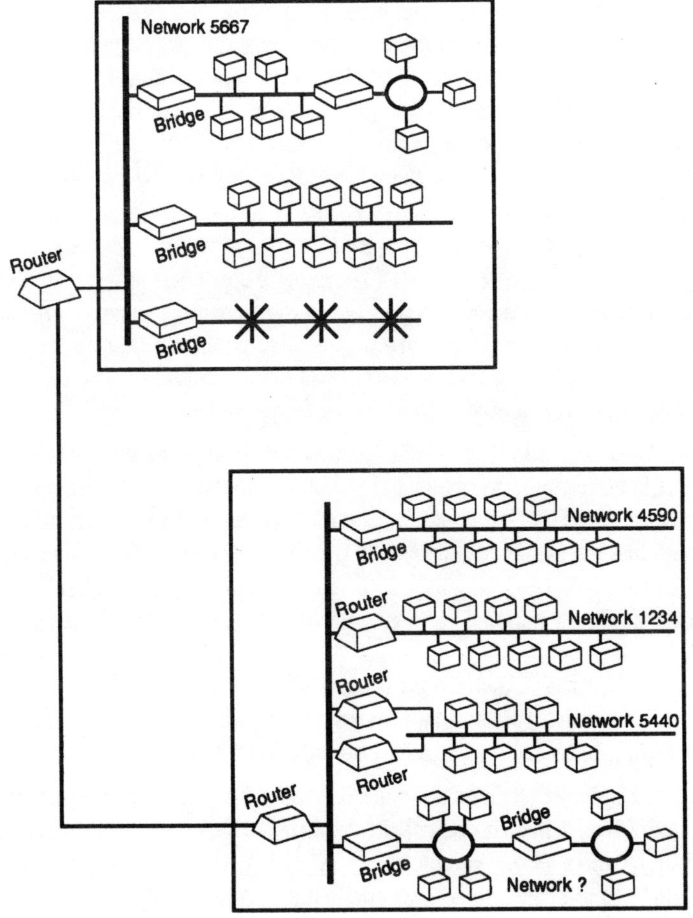

Introducing Gateways

A **gateway** reformats or re-envelopes a packet, performing functions associated with the Network through the Application Layer. (In contrast, a router chooses the best route for a packet but changes only the packet's addressing.) **Architecture gateways** transform packets from one architectural and protocol stack type to another, almost always at the Network Layer. **Application gateways** transform a packet's specific application or presentation format to another, usually at the Application Layer (Layer 7). Many gateways today simply put a new **envelope** around the packet that needs to traverse a "foreign" protocol network. This enveloping process is a popular short-term solution to many protocol incompatibility problems. (The general concept is also referred to as **tunnelling** and **pass-through**. We will see another example of enveloping in Chapter 4.) Re-enveloping is so popular because it is less processing-intensive and therefore less time-consuming. In business terms, performance and throughput improve.

The most common type of wide-area or **external gateway** transforms a packet belonging to one of the popular LAN Network Layer protocols into a CCITT-standard X.25 packet, ready for wide-area packet transmission, and is called an **X.25 gateway**. With an X.25 gateway in place, a LAN can pass packets to remote databases or another LAN connected to a national or international network. The X.25 standard, which has sub-standards covering the Physical through the Network Layers, includes extensive error-handling mechanisms. We'll discuss how companies purchase and manage their wide-area infrastructures, including X.25 packet-transport services, in Chapter 4.

An X.25 gateway can be software resident on a general purpose communications server, a dedicated hardware/software device or a board inserted into a server, switch, router or other LAN citizen. In some extremely time-critical wide-area applications, the individual user devices need their own dedicated access to an X.25 wide-area network through board-level X.25 gateways. Stock and commodity brokers are examples of X.25 board users.

X.25 Gateways

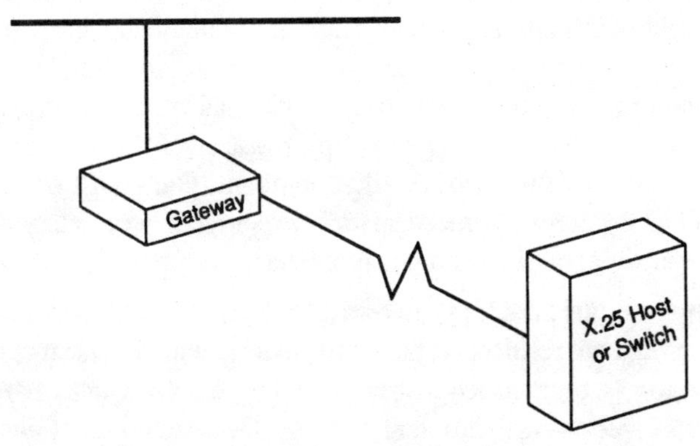

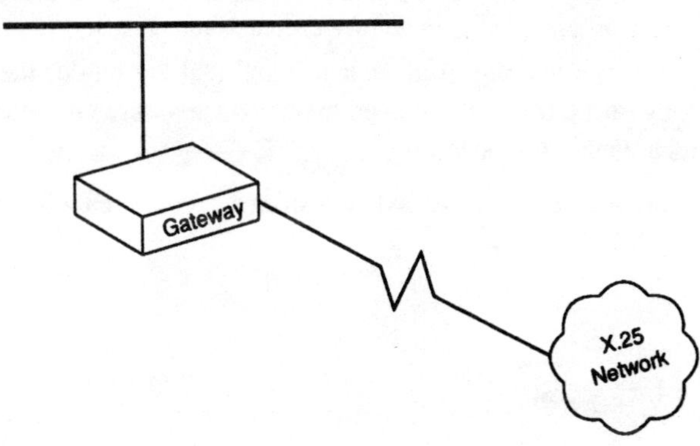

Application and Internal Gateways

The application gateway focuses on re-enveloping and sometimes actually transforming application formats, generally in word processing and electronic mail. A gateway might translate documents from one word-processing package to another (All-In-One to MultiBUS in the illustration) or it might link two electronic mail systems (a proprietary product to standard X.400, for example). Instead of converting your internal mail systems to be X.400-compliant, you could simply use X.400 as the transport mechanism between your proprietary system and your supplier or customer's proprietary system.

An **internal (architecture) gateway** can be used to link two groups of devices that are resident on the same physical wire but use incompatible protocols, for instance DECnet and TCP/IP. Two devices that create packets conforming to different protocol stacks are logically and functionally invisible to each other, regardless of their physical location.

A gateway can either be a stand-alone dedicated platform or it can be software or a board product resident on a multipurpose hardware platform. You could load gateway software onto an existing server, for example. Before you decide to do this, consider the peak loads the server is already experiencing. Also bear in mind that the harder the server works, the more often it will need maintenance and repair. Plan backups and hot standbys accordingly.

In the next chapter we move on to consider the wide-area infrastructure of an internet.

Application Gateways

Server acts as gateway
to two applications on
the same network

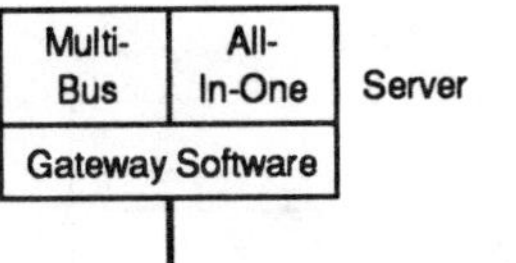

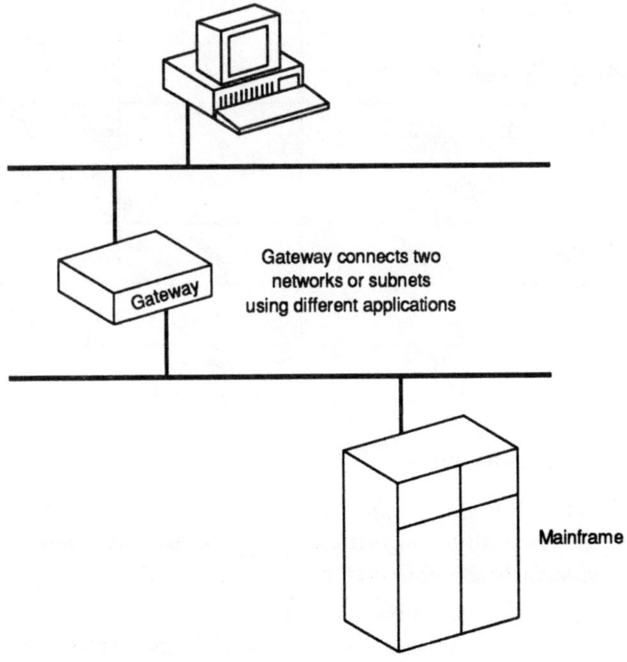

Summary

Bridges vs. Routers

	Bridge	Router
A single LAN	✓	
Segmentation	weak	strong
Filtering	✓	more
Multi-path options		✓
Upper layer protocol-blind	✓	
Traffic management		✓
Improves reliability		✓
Cheap	✓	
Fast	✓	

Gateway Summary

A gateway restructures a packet

- ❒ Architecture gateways frequently use enveloping or tunnelling for efficient transit of foreign-protocol networks
- ❒ Application gateways, as well as architecture gateways can be used within a single network, to translate packets of different formats

Review – Chapter 3

1. What specific business benefits will a routed internet give you?
2. What applications in your company should be part of a routed internet?
3. Routers and end users _______their availability to each other. Describe the 2 most popular methods, step-by-step.
4. How does a router build a dynamic routing table?
5. Routers build logical _______ maps to help them create routes.
6. RIP uses _____ to determine its distance vector to distant networks.
7. The ISO protocols for end user-to-router and router-to-router communication are called _______ and _________, respectively. (Infer from the names.)
8. If your internet devices must be able to route XNS and bridge LAT, you need ______________.
9. If your internet has DECnet routing only and you want to add IP routing capability because your new subsidiary is a TCP/IP installation, what are your options for adding this functionality?
10. What can you do for yourself today to reduce your future internet upgrade costs?
11. An example of a Network Layer gateway is __________.
12. How does an application gateway work?
13. Why would you need to gateway two devices on the same LAN segment?
14. A gateway usually reformats a packet by adding a new ____.
15. Under what circumstances would you consider adding communication gateway software to a server?
16. For what applications would it be wise to give individual end users gateway software?

Key Words

The words and phrases highlighted in **bold** represent key concepts in this chapter. Please take the time now to write down your own definitions of these terms, using the list below and additional paper if needed. Then compare your efforts to the training text. This is an excellent way for you to determine weak points in the breadth and depth of your understanding of this chapter.

router
going off-net
IS
hops
neighbor routers
cost
redundant paths
alternate routes
dotted decimal notation
advertise
backward learning
ES/IS address flooding
routing tables
topology maps
routing protocols
RIP
metric
hop count
routing update
gosip
hybrid internet
bridged LAN
routed internet
integrated bridge/router
unroutable protocols
gateway
architecture gateway
application gateway
envelope
tunnelling
pass-through
external gateway
X.25 gateway
internal (architecture) gateway

4

Wide-Area Internetworking

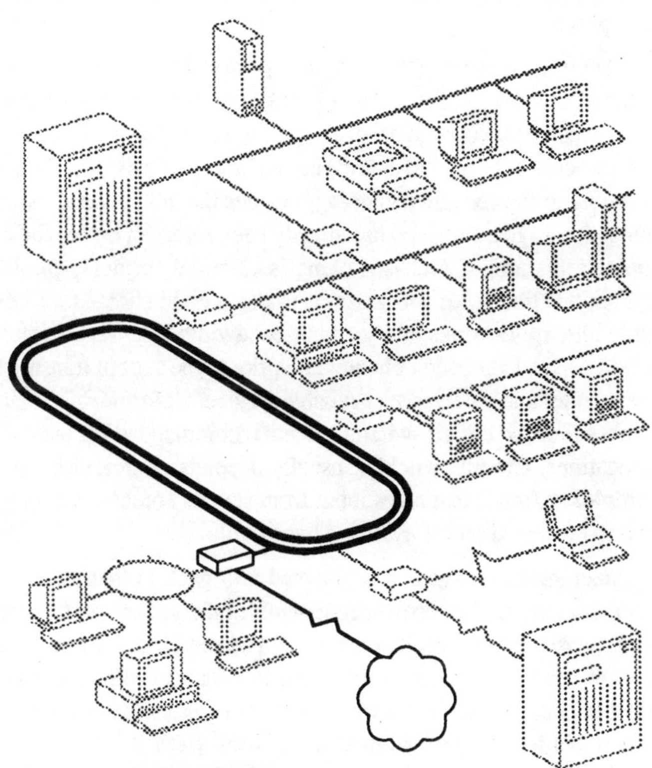

Goals of This Chapter

When you have completed this chapter you should be able to:

- ❐ Understand the difference between circuit- and packet-switching
- ❐ Determine whether your company needs private or hybrid instead of public packet-switching service
- ❐ Understand the technical and business issues associated with T-1 service
- ❐ Discuss your business need and timetable for frame relay, SMDS or SONET migration

Wide-Area Internetworking Technologies

This chapter delves into wide-area internetworking by looking at the wide-area transport technologies and services. The technologies and services we will investigate include some existing and some near-future options.

Let's begin with **circuit switching** and **packet switching.** In a circuit-switched network, a connection (**circuit**) must be set up between sender and receiver before the sender begins to send. This connection creation process (called **call setup**, circuit setup or call establishment, according to the specific technology) means that all the bandwidth the connection is going to need has already been reserved before the communication starts. Circuit-switching is essential for delay-intolerant applications like voice and video. It is also a good choice for variable bandwidth applications and for high-bandwidth LAN-LAN internetworking. The dedication of bandwidth prior to the start of transmission gives sender and receiver very reliable service. Unfortunately, call setup takes time, so circuit switching is not recommended for bursty data applications. Circuit switching usually depends on a device called a **multiplexer** (mux) that takes input from several sources and arranges for it to be shared on the available bandwidth.

In packet-switching, data is segmented into packets that are sent out into the internet. The receiver re-assembles the packets in the correct order, recreating the original message. The sender and receiver don't allocate bandwidth before they begin to communicate, so a packet-switching network can experience lost packets due to intermittent congestion, but it is very frugal in its use of bandwidth.

Packet and Circuit Switching

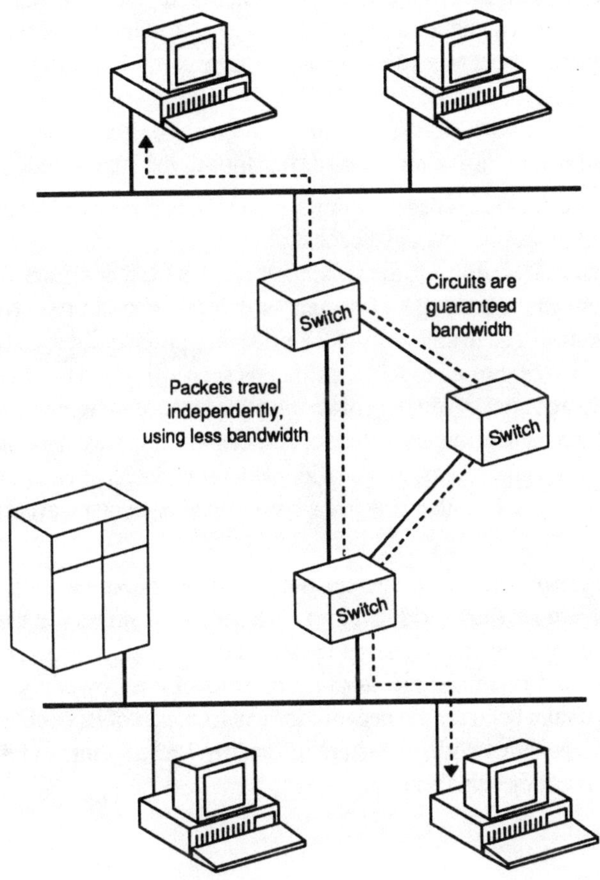

Public, Private and Hybrid Networks

Packet wide-area internet bandwidth can either be a service that you buy as-needed from a **public packet vendor** like Infonet or it can be an infrastructure of your own packet switches. If you buy your packet services from a public packet vendor, you pay a monthly bill based on the number of packets you generate for transport. This is the lowest-cost solution for companies with relatively low usage or for companies with many small offices (with only one or two computers) scattered throughout the country; auto dealerships fit the latter profile.

If you decide to create your own private network, you will buy and install packet switches in the locations you want to link, arrange to bring your LAN traffic into the switches through a local link, then lease communication bandwidth for your switch-to-switch traffic. This bandwidth will be available from long-distance providers at speeds ranging from 9600 bps up to 45 Mbps. In this scenario, you have total ownership and control of your communications infrastructure; you also have all the management and service responsibilities. This solution appeals to many companies as their wide-area traffic increases and as they establish LANs (rather than just a few isolated computers) at each remote site.

The final option is an attempt to have the best of both worlds: a **virtual private network** (VPN). A long-distance carrier offers you the guaranteed capacity you would get from owning a private network, with none of the service and maintenance responsibilities, by carving out the equivalent of a private network for you from part of its public switched telephone network. VPNs are offered by MCI, Sprint, and AT&T, as well as other smaller companies.

Public, Private and Hybrid Networks

Who needs public packet networking?

- ❑ Many scattered locations
- ❑ Bursty traffic at a low level (updating the database once a day, for example)
- ❑ No LAN-to-LAN traffic; PC-to-mainframe or PC-to-LAN connections
- ❑ No desire to manage the WAN

Who needs a private network?

- ❑ Phone bill over $10,000/month
- ❑ High data traffic levels
  - ❑ video, animation
  - ❑ high % of color graphics workstations on site
  - ❑ locations with LANs, not isolated PCs
- ❑ Significant amount of international LAN-to-LAN traffic AND a desire to negotiate with foreign carriers
- ❑ Willing to hiring adequate management staff
- ❑ Able to afford capital outlay, maintenance, upgrades

Who needs a hybrid network?

- ❑ You fit the private network profile
- ❑ But you don't want capital costs or management responsibility

T-1 Service

If you are interested in at least one Mbps of bandwidth for your wide-area internetworking, investigate **T-1 service**, which corresponds to telephony's digital signal level 1 (**DS-1**). Because it is a circuit-switched service, T-1 terminology comes from telephony rather than data communications.

T-1 service is usually sold **subrated**, that is, composed of 24 DS-0 channels carrying data, voice or video traffic plus one 8 Kb channel carrying signalling information. Since the 8 Kb channel is part of the T-1 pipe, we say signalling is **in-band**. Each **DS-0 channel** is a 64 Kb voice-grade channel, with 56 Kb available for use and the remaining 8 Kb allocated for per-channel in-band signalling.

The T-1 service equals 1.544 Mbps in the United States, Japan and South Korea and 2.048 Mbps in the rest of the world (the **CEPT** – European networking – standard). How many DS-0s does the CEPT standard equal?

T-1 service can also be **unsubrated**, in which case the entire T-1 bandwidth is available for allocation as needed. This **bandwidth on demand** means that the T-1 multiplexer allocates bandwidth as each incoming application needs it: video needs much more bandwidth than voice, for example. If you buy T-1 muxes and set up a private network, you still need to lease your T-1 wide-area trunks from a long-distance provider. You can also lease a fraction of a T-1, subrated into DS-0s. This is called **fractional T-1 service.**

T-1

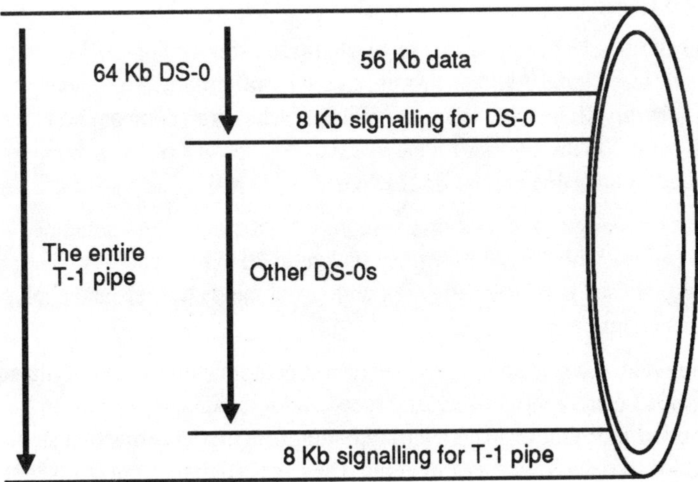
64 Kb DS-0
56 Kb data
8 Kb signalling for DS-0
The entire T-1 pipe
Other DS-0s
8 Kb signalling for T-1 pipe

T-1 Components

A **Channel Service Unit** (CSU) provides an interface between the T-1 signalling and the local loop (the wire between your premises and the local telco exchange). The **Digital Service Unit** (DSU) has a parallel function; it converts RS-232-C or other terminal-oriented signalling into a DS-1 signal. T-1 muxes almost universally have integrated CSUs and DSUs.

In the illustration, you can see a **channel bank** turning analog voice calls into digital output (a process called **companding**). Computer data is already digital so it is easy to multiplex data with companded voice. If your T-1 mux doesn't have a CSU/DSU integrated in its box, you need to have an external CSU/DSU.

A promising new business development is the rapid deployment of **T-3** service with 44.736 Mbps, equivalent to 28 T-1s. Generally T-3 service is used in private networks with unsubrated channels and sophisticated muxes.

Telephone service providers are becoming more interested in **digitized voice** because of the increased speed and reliability of digitally-transmitted information. The telcos' creation of a digital infrastructure includes the deployment of Integrated Services Digital Networks (**ISDN**) and Synchronous Optical Network (**SONET**) services, now under way world-wide. (We'll return to SONET later in this chapter.) ISDN is an international standard for an integrated voice/data/video service that is slowly becoming available from local telcos.

Evolution of T-1 Components

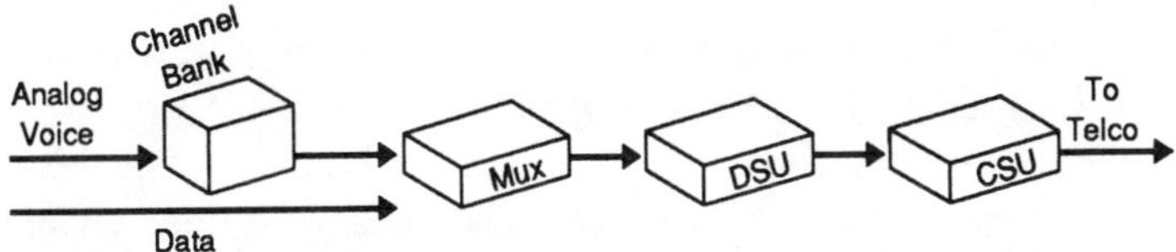

or

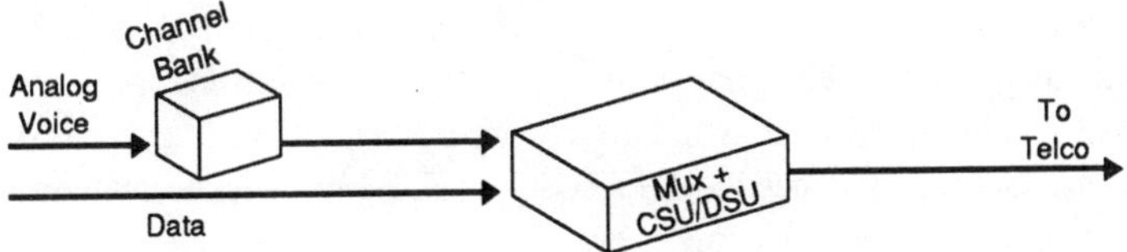

Integrating T-1 Backbones into LAN Infrastructures

Network managers originally bought T-1 muxes to lower the costs of their voice networks and to improve the reliability of both voice and data transmission. In the 1990s, the percentage of data carried over T-1 pipes continues to increase every year.

If your wide-area internetwork uses T-1 muxes to connect LANs, each mux has a series of wide-area network (WAN) ports and LAN ports, supporting many media choices. You can add a bridge or router board to these muxes and have full-fledged LAN internetworking without adding an additional box. Alliances between internet and LAN vendors will lead to more of these integrations as time goes on. An advantage of adding a bridge/router board to an existing T-1 infrastructure, besides the lower expense, is that the integrated box can be managed from a single console.

Network managers believe that they need more wide-area options, specifically faster speeds and more cost-effective solutions. Although X.25 wide-area packet switching is very reliable, it isn't very speedy. What users seem to need is the speediness of T-1 in a packet-switching, not circuit-switching, technology.

One option is to internetwork at a lower layer, before X.25's Network Layer error control comes into play. That is exactly what internetwork designers have done, in a new Data Link Layer internetworking technology called **frame relay.** The essence of frame relay internetworking is that frames are pushed along through a wide-area infrastructure, with as little processing as possible at each switch point. This lack of processing makes frame relay very speedy. Let's take an in-depth look at this new technology now.

Frame Relay Networking

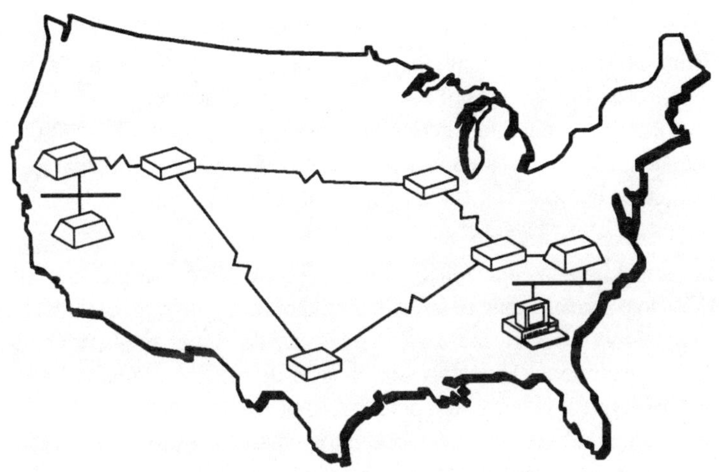

 Router on User LAN

 Frame Relay Node

Enveloping

Frame Relay Envelope	IP Packet	Frame Relay Envelope

Choosing Frame Relay

In order to benefit from frame relay technology, your application must use nearly error-free transmission lines, must not be delay-sensitive and must allow the ultimate sender and receiver to handle higher-level error control. This means that voice, video, 9.6 kbps dialup lines and dumb terminals need not apply. Can you see why this must be so?

Think about the Data Link Layer. The other Data Link Layer device we've examined in this book – the bridge – can filter very cleverly but essentially is limited to filtering or forwarding, a simple GO-NO GO decision. That is the essence of the second OSI layer. Error checking is limited to determining bit errors. More complex error checking requires the upper layers of software.

In current implementations, the frame relay switch's response to a bad FCS, to congestion and to any other kind of question or problem is the same: throw it out! Because frame relay puts the responsibility for end-to-end error control squarely on the shoulders of the ultimate sender and receiver, it is most suitable for LAN/LAN traffic, where devices are using sophisticated network error control protocols (Layers 3 through 7 in the typical architecture).

The **Data Link Connection Identifier** (DLCI) is the **virtual circuit number** associated with the destination router port. A frame relay network's architecture involves a **permanent virtual circuit** (PVC) set up between two routers and a DLCI associated with the PVC. Each frame that the router sends off to the frame relay switch has a DLCI that determines how it is routed through the frame relay network. These switches use very simple translation and routing tables to pass a frame from port to port in the network until it reaches its destination. The routers have an internal translation table that translates DLCIs into whatever local and network addressing scheme the LAN uses. In effect the frame relay formatting becomes the envelope that the router puts the user packet into for wide-area transport.

The ultimate simplicity of the frame relay concept is also its greatest weakness. Since the nodes do NOT communicate with each other as LAN routers do, they cannot tell each other about congestion they may be experiencing. To deal with this weakness, several additions to the ANSI/CCITT standard frame relay specification have been proposed.

Frame Relay

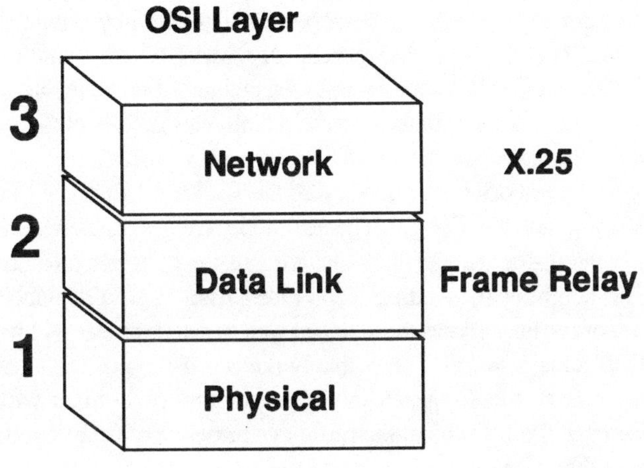

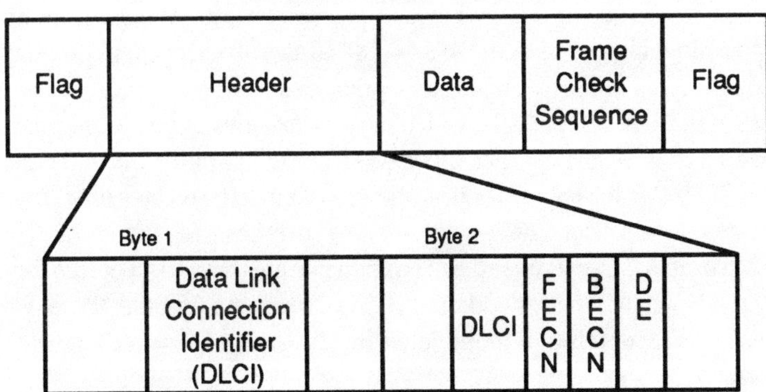

"Data" can be a complete TCP/IP packet. If an entire packet does not fit, the router will fragment it into multiple frames. The router is responsible for packet reassembly at the destination.

Congestion Management

In the illustration opposite you can see that a DLCI on the middle node has become congested. It is attempting to communicate this problem to its upstream and downstream neighbors on that DLCI by using the optional **BECN** and **FECN** bits, respectively. Every time a frame on the DLCI destined for Network 2 passes the congested node, the node activates the Forward Explicit Congestion Notification (FECN) bit in that frame. The congested node can do the same when it encounters a frame going in the opposite direction, using the Backward Explicit Correction Notification (BECN) bit. The next node will see the BECN bit set to 1 instead of 0 and understand that it is causing congestion for its immediate neighbor by sending it too many frames. It will reduce the amount of traffic it allows through and wait to see if the BECN bit continues to remain set. You've probably noticed the major weakness of this approach: the congested node cannot initiate contact with its neighbors, but must rely on the fortuitous presence of frames going in the right direction.

Other optional features that a vendor can implement are the **Discard Eligibility** (DE) bit and the **Committed Information Rate** (CIR). Less-important traffic, or traffic from bandwidth-hogs, have DE bits set so these frames can be dropped when congestion begins to build. This allows more important traffic to flow and allows all users approximately equal access to the available bandwidth. Users can also specify an average traffic level, the CIR, which the network tries to guarantee a user access to. If a user exceeds this throughput temporarily, the nodes set the DE bit on the excess frames, allowing them to be thrown out if congestion exists. The CIR mechanism also specifies a maximum rate for each user. All frames over the maximum rate are thrown out before they actually get into the network, protecting throughput for other users. We discuss frame relay in more detail in *Mastering Advanced Internetworking*.

Explicit Congestion Management

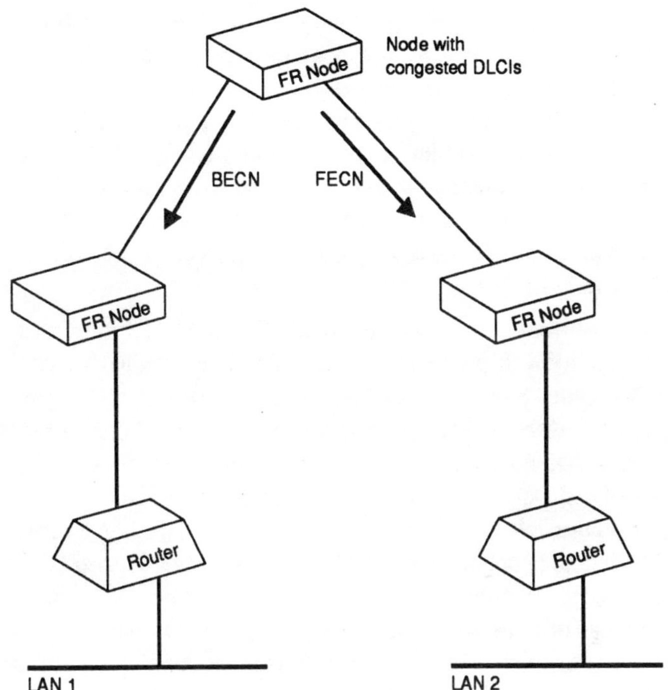

High Bandwidth Transport

Bellcore developed and ANSI has approved a new digital fiber optics technology for both wide-area and local networking, called SONET. Telephone companies and other common carriers have embraced it heartily for long distance as well as local telco operations. SONET design reflects T-3-sized building blocks. As you can see from the chart opposite, SONET boasts very high transmission rates. The service name (**optical carrier**) has a corresponding signalling designation (**synchronous transport signal**). **OC-1** and **OC-3** infrastructures are being deployed now and additional levels are in lab and theoretical development, from STS-48 at 2.48832 Gigabits/second (Gbps) to STS-255 at 132.191 Gbps.

Many WAN vendors are investigating OC-1 and OC-3 interfaces for future addition to product offerings. The international version of SONET, called Synchronous Digital Hierarchy (**SDH**), is being investigated by WAN vendors who do substantial international business. Although SONET is currently competing for buyer attention with other Physical and Data Link Layer protocols, especially FDDI (Fiber Distributed Data Interface, ANSI's 100 Mbps standard), frame relay, B-ISDN and Bellcore's Switched Multimegabit Data Service (**SMDS**) over DQDB (Distributed Queue Dual Bus),we can expect that ultimately one of them will become the most popular standard for wide-area infrastructures while another will grab the high ground in local internetworking. Most analysts expect SONET to become popular as a backbone and wide-area technology, while the to-the-desktop market will belong to other protocols.

Let's move on now to the sometimes herculean job of managing an internetwork.

SONET Data Rates

OC Optical Carrier	STS Synch Transport Signal	Line Rates (Mbps)
OC-1	STS-1	51.84
OC-3	STS-3	155.52
OC-12	STS-12	622.08
OC-48	STS-48	2488.32

Summary

- Packet switching is available through public network vendors, as a private network owned and managed by your staff or as a virtual private network. Standard X.25 packet switching is reliable, but slow.
- T-1 service delivers a 1.544 Mbps service and can be part of both public and private networks. T-1 muxes with integrated LAN bridges and routers and CSU/DSUs are becoming more popular.
- Frame relay networking is Data Link Layer networking for the wide-area. It can deliver significant speed increases compared to X.25 networking but depends on endpoint devices to handle error control.
- Synchronous optical networking (SONET) offers bandwidths of up to 622 Mbps. Other high-bandwidth WAN options are SMDS and ISDN.

Review – Chapter 4

1. What are some of the advantages of T-1 networking for LAN/LAN networking?
2. What kinds of companies should consider public packet switching networks for their wide-area infrastructure?
3. If you depend on call setups prior to beginning to communicate, you are using ________-switching.
4. Bandwidth ____________ means that each application can capture as much bandwidth as it needs.
5. DS-0s have a total bandwidth of ________ and a usable bandwidth of _________ because they include signalling bandwidth of __________.
6. T-1 signalling is ____-band.
7. The DS-1 signal level is _________ Mbps in the Netherlands and _______ Mbps in Sri Lanka.
8. DS-1 carries _______ DS-0s in the U.S.
9. For frame relay networking to be appropriate, what three elements must your wide-area networking architecture include?

    ____

10. Describe how frame relay deals with congestion in the network.
11. The frame relay address is called a _______________.
12. What are the most popular SONET optical carrier levels called?
13. What applications in your company would be likely to benefit from high-bandwidth WAN service?
14. Do you plan to create a private metropolitan area network (MAN) or will you subscribe to a public MAN? What factors will most influence your decision?

Key Words

The words and phrases highlighted in **bold** represent key concepts in this chapter. Please take the time now to write down your own definitions of these terms, using the list below and additional paper if needed. Then compare your efforts to the training text. This is an excellent way for you to determine weak points in the breadth and depth of your understanding of this chapter.

circuit switching
packet switching
circuit
call setup
multiplexer
public packet vendor
virtual private network
T-1 service
DS-1
subrated
in-band
DS-0 channel
CEPT
unsubrated
bandwidth on demand
fractional T-1 service
Channel Service Unit
Digital Service Unit
channel bank
companding
ISDN
SONET
frame relay
Data Link Connection Identifier
virtual circuit number
permanent virtual circuit
BECN and FECN
DE and CIR
optical carrier
synchronous transport signal
OC-1 and OC-3
SDH
SMDS

5
Network Management

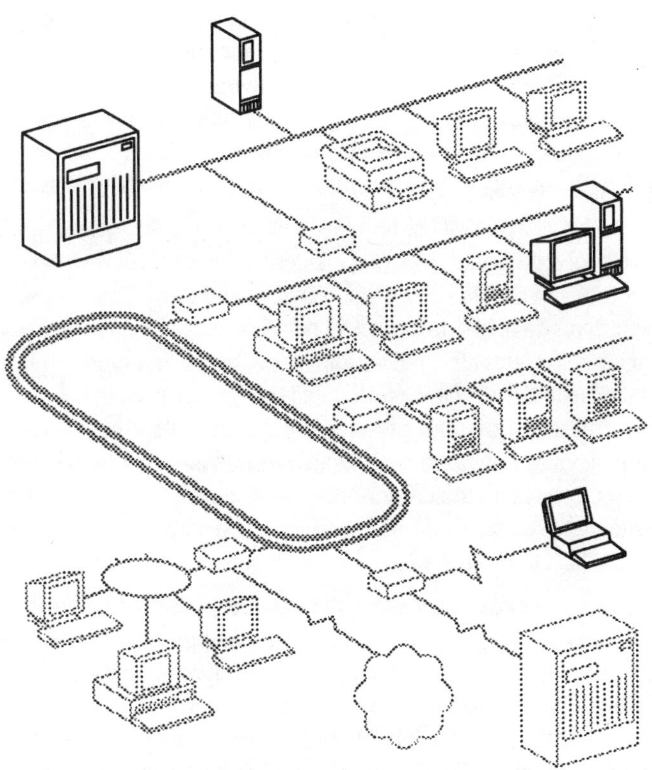

Goals of this Chapter

When you have successfully completed this chapter, you will:

- ❒ Understand the need for effective management of your company's network infrastructure
- ❒ Understand the five classes of OSI Management
- ❒ Be prepared to choose a network management architecture and develop a strategy for staged implementation of that architecture
- ❒ Be ready to use protocol analyzers and other tools for software management

For a detailed course focusing exclusively on internetwork management, see *Mastering Network Management* in this series.

Why Manage Your Internetwork?

Do you think of your network as a focus for cost-containment? Don't be too quick to wield the ax. Spending money on good network management will reduce your costs without affecting your ability to deliver state-of-the-art service to the end users. Do you think of your network as a strategic tool in your ultimate battle for market share? Do you visualize your network infrastructure as a vital corporate asset, delivering direct business dividends far beyond its costs? Even better! You already understand that a reliable information infrastructure is second only to the quality of your people as your ultimate business asset.

Network management has become much more challenging as networks have evolved into internetworks. Internet devices link networks composed of thousands of end-user devices and these end-user devices themselves have had an impact on network management. Workstations – with color, graphics, animation, video, audio and other high-bandwidth capabilities – have proliferated through networks, in some cases replacing less-powerful personal computers. These new high-bandwidth devices produce more overall traffic and they do so in bursty, unpredictable ways. In addition, new applications involve more server interactions, as more end-users take advantage of increased opportunities for information-sharing.

As end-users make better use of the information infrastructure, they are also making greater demands of the infrastructure. A poorly managed infrastructure may not be able to continue delivering reliable service as service needs skyrocket. The burgeoning use of client/server computing architectures stems at least in part from a desire to reduce network clogging and postpone a migration to higher-bandwidth media.

In some cases, more or higher-powered internet devices will solve "the problem." Most of the time, better management tools are needed.

Why Network Management?

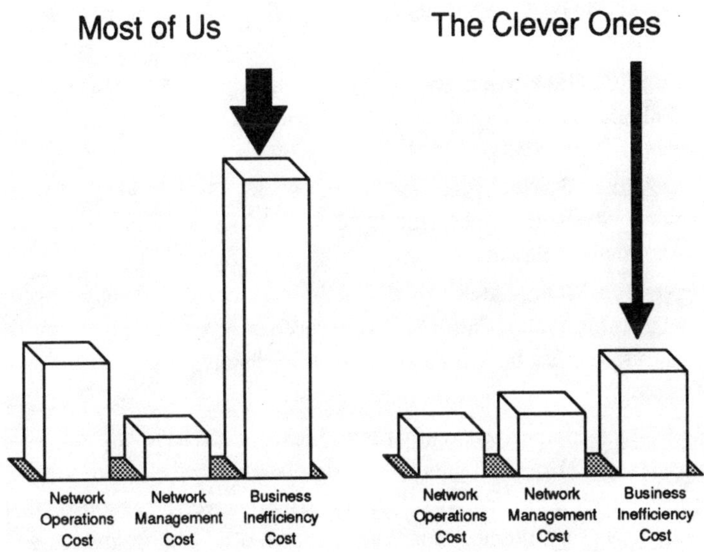

Invest in your infrastructure and set your people free to produce market share results. Research studies have shown that every dollar you invest in network management yields between $5–12 in business benefits.

Network Management Functions

The OSI Network Management standards committees have divided the needed functions into five categories.

- **Fault Management**: Notification of failures and faults in network devices: what's broken and where it is.
- **Performance Management**: How well is the network using its available bandwidth? What is the percentage of uptime?
- **Configuration Management**: How quickly do you learn about inadvertent configuration changes? How quickly can you implement planned new configurations?
- **Accounting Management**: Charge-backs to individual departments; measures of utilization of network bandwidth by various communities of users.
- **Security Management**: How well do you control who has access to what information? Information, because it is a strategic corporate resource, must be safeguarded from intrusions, both internal and external.

Fault Management and Configuration Management have generated the most significant cost savings to date, simply because they represent primarily Physical Layer (Layer 1) functions. Some vendors estimate that 70 to 80% of an internet's total management need can be summarized as cable plant management. For each device in your internet, you need real-time answers to the questions: Has it failed? Where is it physically? Real-time management of your physical plant is your essential first step, regardless of your network type, size or geographic location.

Performance Management measures how well a device is performing its functions; a good product here can give you early warning of impending failures. Because it involves software as well as hardware, we can say that Performance Management has moved further up the OSI Model from the physical plant concerns. Surveys of network managers show security and accounting (Application Layer concerns) last on their list of needs.

OSI Network Management Functions

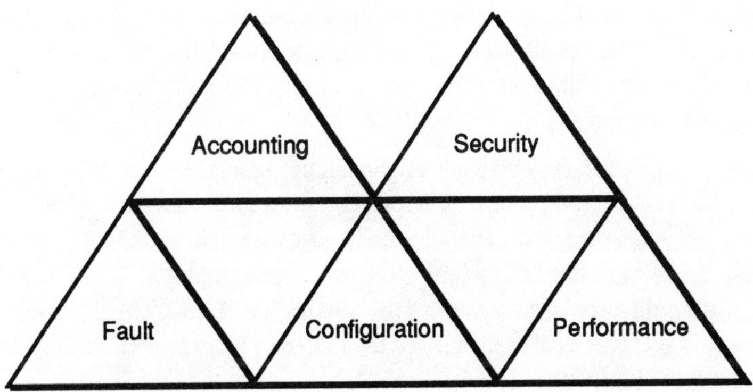

Management Marketplace

A management **architecture** is a multilayered model into which specific management **protocols** fit. Each architecture has a specific design philosophy, which includes the kinds of problems it is optimized to help solve or the types of networks it is optimized to manage. Manager software resident in the network manager communicates with devices (**clients**) in the internet through software **agents**. Managed nodes include **managed objects**: remote connections, routing tables, interfaces, counters and flags.

Let's take a quick look at the management marketplace, focusing on the two most important standards. At present, most internetworking device vendors sell some sort of management software. The standard protocols that we are discussing here were developed so that network managers could create an infrastructure using devices from different vendors and still be able to manage their internet from a single management station. This noble goal is still not a reality – but standards are always a good place to start.

The Internet community developed the **Simple Network Management Protocol** (SNMP) primarily for TCP/IP environments and almost exclusively for managing the internetworking infrastructure itself. The OSI Network Management committees developed the Common Management Interface Specification (CMIS), the **Common Management Interface Protocol** (CMIP) and **CMIP Over TCP** (CMOT) for management of all device types. The new CMIP Over Logical Link (CMOL) standard allows designers to manage "short stacks" – relatively simple networks with Applications Layer software directly over the LLC sublayer. SNMP focuses its attention on the management of relatively low-level objects, primarily counters. The CMIP interface, in contrast, is more far-reaching and allows applications to perform control and event reporting as well as monitoring.

Managers, Managed Nodes and Managed Objects

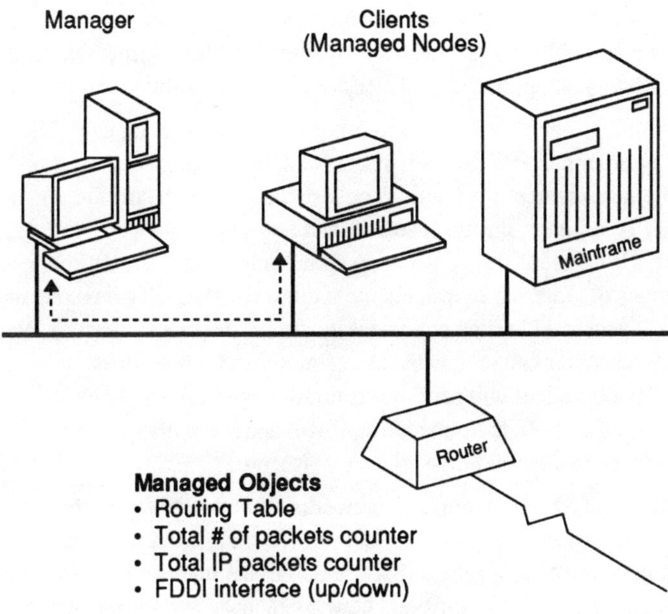

Managers communicate with the clients' user agents to share information on managed objects within each client.

Proxy Agents: Linking SNMP and CMIP

SNMP enjoys one significant advantage over CMIP when implemented in internet devices: it requires much less memory and processing because it rarely initiates actions unless an active problem area that generates an **alert** exists. If the management application has to take a certain action as soon as a counter exceeds a threshold, the manager must continually poll the agent, at shorter and shorter intervals as the alert threshold approaches, to retrieve the current value.

In contrast, since CMIP puts the full protocol on the node agent's side, the agent acts as a full partner, instead of simply responding to requests. If the management application requests updates on a specific counter every 10 minutes, the agent sets a timer and sends a packet to the manager with current status at the specified intervals, until the manager changes the interval or cancels the request for status. This means that CMIP generates less management traffic for the same activities. Network managers can set custom alert conditions for specific devices and the device's agent will send status updates to the manager every time the alert threshold is reached. The CMIP agent can also perform complex tasks like rebuilding a routing table.

CMIP- and SNMP-dominated networks can manage each other's devices through a **proxy agent**. The proxy is implemented in software that acts as an intermediate between a device managed by a foreign protocol (a completely different network management protocol or simply another vendor's implementation of the same protocol) and the network manager. Both architectures include storage of management data in a **Management Information Base** (MIB), although the internal structures differ. CMIP/CMOT can store complex data objects (arrays, tables, etc.) and it supports OSI's accounting and network configuration options.

If your network uses intelligent hubs, the user agents, including proxies, reside on the hub rather than on the individual user devices.

Comparing SNMP And CMIP

SNMP	CMIP
Simple data types only	Complex, custom data types possible
Suitable primarily for internet devices	Suitable for computers, workstations, servers
Monitoring, some control	Monitoring, control, accounting
Manager polls; Agent responds	Agent can initiate interactions and respond to complex commands
Heavily loaded LANs may be impacted by constant SNMP polling packets	A lost management packet can confuse manager when follow-ups arrive
Optimized for TCP/UDP, but can be used with other network types	Designed for generic use across all networks and devices

Build Your Pyramid

It simply isn't possible to manage user devices, the internet infrastructure, LAN wiring and complex software at every layer with one management protocol or even one set of tools. Your best strategy is to pinpoint your own most significant problem areas and begin to apply proactive dollars to preventing these problems. (Keep in mind as you begin this exercise that you are undoubtedly spending a lot of money as a corporation through lack of reliability. These dollars are real dollars; factor them into your decisions.)

- EVERYone needs good cable management
- Almost everyone needs good server management
- Many networks need internet infrastructure management
- Some networks need reliable WAN links
- Some networks experience persistent software problems because of incompatible releases or multi-vendor headaches
- Some networks have electronic mail problems

Figure out what the core business of your company is and see to it that your network management strategy protects it. Discover the key applications and who uses them; make sure you deliver reliable service to these users and applications. Following the core business applications, go after the key productivity activities. If the company falls apart without its e-mail, that makes e-mail reliability a high priority for you. Keep your focus on your company's true business, don't over-focus on accounting and you'll save a lot of money in the long term.

Unfortunately, no one kind of management system will solve all your problems so you will need to invest in a variety of tools in more than one category. If you are managing a network for a Fortune 500 corporation, you will find most of your benefits in an architecture that allows you to keep a centralized record of all network activities and also allows you to interrogate distributed devices.

Building Your Pyramid

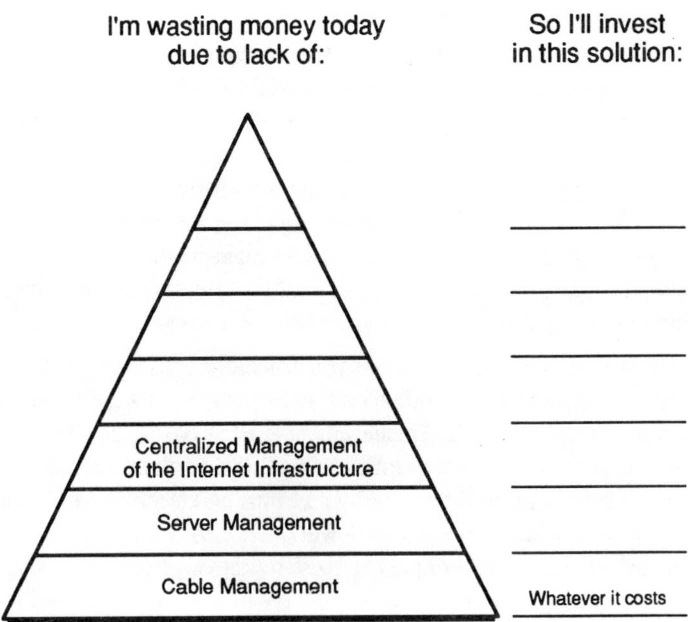

Management of Software Layers

To diagnose software problems in the Data Link through Application Layers, invest in protocol analyzers: portable or desktop computers that copy packets for management analysis. You can program sampling for specific packet types (by length, Network Layer protocol, broadcasts, and so on) or for specific sender or receiver addresses. As you collect data, you can display it and develop conclusions. Since the analyzer copies the entire packet into its memory, you can dissect the offending packets in detail, layer by layer, until you discover the problem area. These analyzers can be portable tools, attached and detached to solve specific problems. Alternatively, you can assign analyzers to each LAN or LAN segment in your internet and dynamically control their sampling operation from a central network management station. In this case, the analyzer would be inactive until the central management station wants to investigate a possible problem on a specific segment.

Some management software helps you manage applications, while network operating systems (NOSs) exist to help you manage sessions and servers. The physical plant management issues have already been discussed. The architecture specifies how all these sources of management information will be coordinated into an effective whole and displayed on a single management workstation. At present, integrated network management (bringing all these sources together onto a single screen in a single format) is rarely possible in a multi-vendor internet. Integrated network management is the essential goal of the next evolutionary stage of internetworking.

Management of internets will become more complex as internets become more complex, but you can ameliorate this trend with thoughtful investment in tools. The remainder of the 1990s will bring an avalanche of new and more sophisticated tools, some of which depend on artificial intelligence. Investment in powerful tools can yield powerful results.

Using Distributed Protocol Analyzers

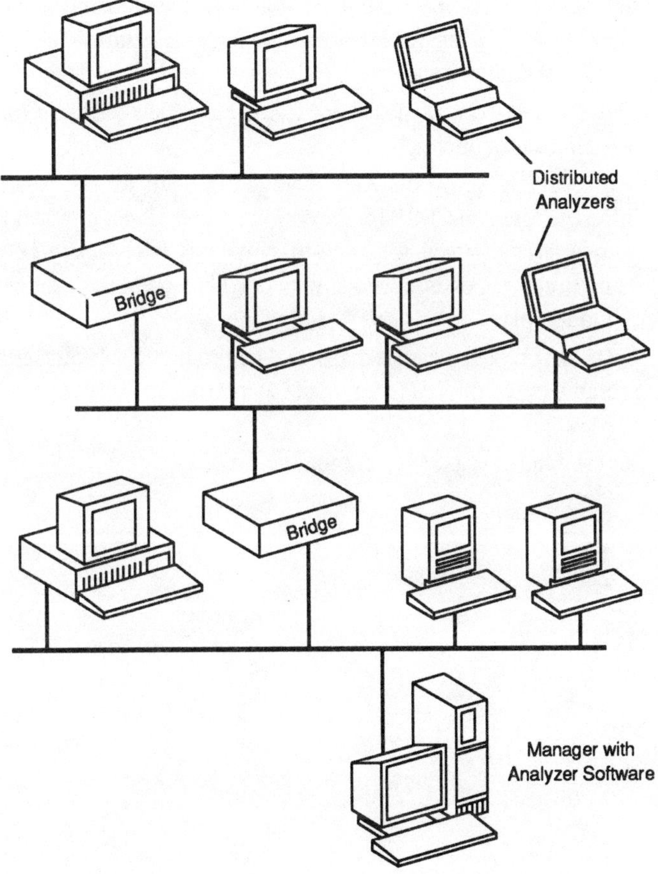

Summary

- A poorly-managed network drains your resources and cripples your employees' productivity. A well-managed network is your second most significant corporate resource.
- Effective network management begins with a well-managed cable plant. Software management and performance tuning are your next most critical issues.
- The OSI Network Management teams have identified five functional areas for attention.
- Two standard protocols have emerged: SNMP for the internet infrastructure and CMIP for the entire network. Each protocol has unique strengths and weaknesses; neither is intrinsically better. The choice depends on your network characteristics and your migration plans.
- Software problems can be diagnosed by protocol analyzers, either portable or distributed throughout the internet and interrogated as needed.
- Invest in tools as part of your internet strategy.

Review – Chapter 5

1. Name the 5 classes of OSI network management.
2. Describe what they cover in terms of your network. What would each allow you to do?
3. What 2 or 3 areas will you focus your network management efforts on? (Cable management is a given.)
4. An SNMP MIB requires every element in an array to be individually fetched, while CMIP allows you to create and fetch complex data types. What are some implications for network management? Consider speed of access, amount of memory, complexity of the code needed to create MIB routines, etc.
5. List at least 5 typical objects and the kind of information you would be likely to store for that object.
6. Describe the difference between a management protocol and a management architecture.
7. Do you think SNMP is an appropriate protocol for your network? Do you prefer a proprietary protocol or CMIP? WHY? (Hint: "Everyone else is buying it" is not a good reason.)
8. Protocol analyzers focus primarily on _____ (software/hardware) problems.
9. If you want to use a distributed scheme of protocol analyzers to focus on Layer 2 problems, you need one analyzer per _______ (LAN/segment/internet).
10. Why is integrated network management so important to you? Why do you think the industry can't offer it to you yet? (Write this out. It will help you to clarify your thinking.)

Key Words

The words and phrases highlighted in **bold** represent key concepts in this chapter. Please take the time now to write down your own definitions of these terms, using the list below and additional paper if needed. Then compare your efforts to the training text. This is an excellent way for you to determine weak points in the breadth and depth of your understanding of this chapter.

fault management
performance management
configuration management
accounting management
security management
architecture
protocols
clients
agents
managed objects
Simple Network Management Protocol
Common Management Interface Protocol
CMIP over TCP
alert
proxy agent
management information base

6

The Future of Internetworking

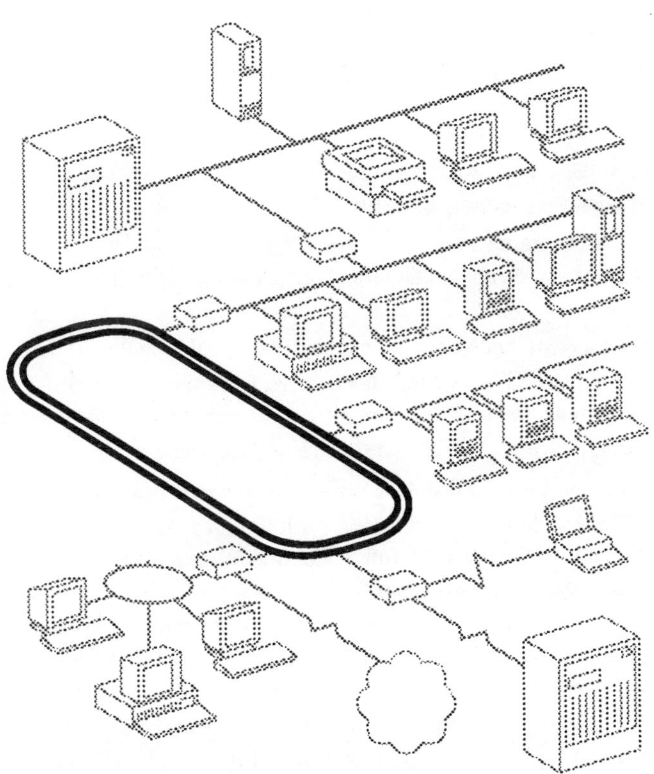

Goals Of This Chapter

When you complete this chapter, you will be able to:

- ❐ Develop your own ideas about probable future directions in products and services
- ❐ Develop a training strategy for your future networking education

The Future of Internetworking Products

There are at least as many answers to this question as there are vendors with "visions" and network managers with problems to solve. Some of the answers also deal with areas beyond the scope of this book–advanced routing algorithms, for example. Assuming that we must focus only on the products and services discussed in this book, here are some of the clearest trends:

- The isolated LAN is becoming an endangered species. Most LANs are now part of internets.
- Internets are becoming more complex, in numbers of infrastructure devices, in the complexity of their topologies and in the power of the applications running on them.
- Internets are now critical to the corporate bottom line. They carry core business applications and safeguard critical business operations.
- Internets are becoming chaotic and less reliable in those companies that have NOT invested in effective integrated network management tools. Internets need more centralized purchasing and management, to lower costs and to streamline procurement.

The future of internetworking products and services, of course, cannot be divorced from the continuing evolution of LAN wiring platforms and basic applications. (A full discussion of these topics is contained in *Mastering Local Area Networks.*) While traditional topologies and media are experiencing relatively restrained growth, intelligent hub sales are skyrocketing. In a similar vein, the intense interest in migrating 100 Mbps FDDI and other sophisticated lower-layer protocols to UTP media is just a small part of a massive potential movement of platforms and applications. The evolution of LAN access is moving rapidly away from uncentralized buses and rings toward concentrators, smart hubs and other easily-managed entities connected through more complex, hierarchical mixed topologies.

LAN Evolution

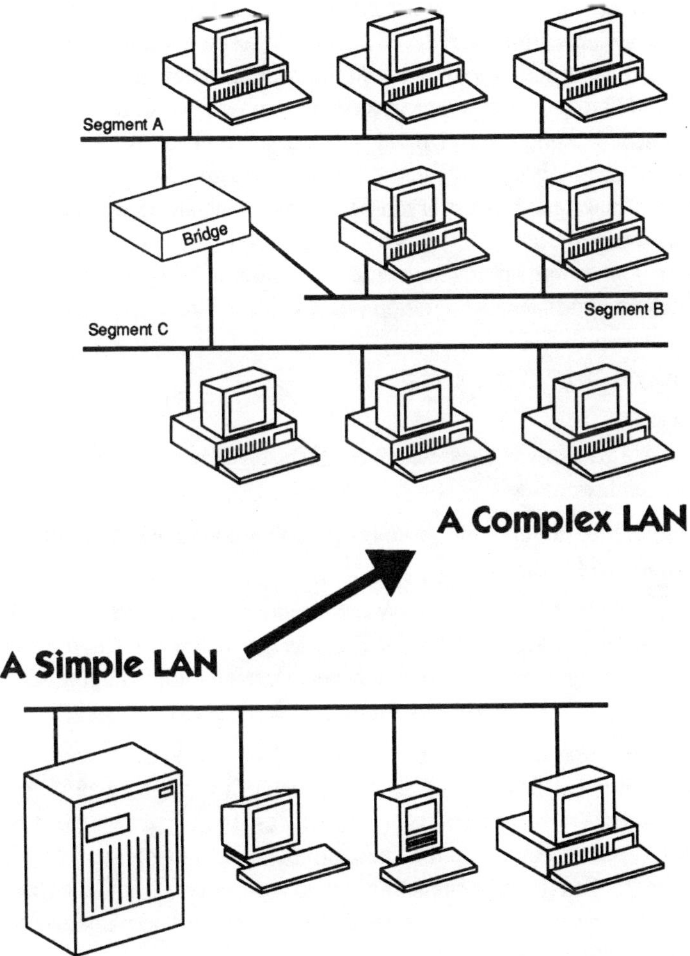

Bridges, Routers and Gateways

Bridging, routing and gateway functionality is evolving rapidly, with both faster hardware platforms and more powerful software. Faster hardware depending on reduced instruction set computing (**RISC**), embedded chips and more powerful processors is a key selling factor in low-end bridge sales, where vendors are primarily competing on price and speed. Another clear trend in bridging and routing platforms is their continuing integration into a single package. Integrated bridge/routers make good financial sense for network managers who expect to integrate unroutable protocols into their existing network, or who have or will have multi-protocol internets. In addition, bridging and routing software continues its migration (via boards or software) into untraditional devices, including

- muxes (T-1/T-3 and other types)
- PBXs
- WAN packet switches, which are themselves being integrated into other devices

Migratable, integratable products probably constitute the strongest buyer need for the 1990s.

One of the critical disadvantages of routing compared to bridging–its cost–will become less important as the decade matures. Prices for routing will drop as router companies develop technology-sharing deals with the major LAN and WAN hub manufacturers.

Users have been embracing both standards-based products and products that allow them to extend the lifetime of existing network infrastructures. Tunnelling has been emerging as the preferred method for relatively fast deployment of new protocols into existing networks. Gateways that focus on tunnelling across architecture boundaries have been experiencing booming sales and this trend will accelerate as the 1990s continue. The deployment of the SR-TB standard into bridging software will allow faster, less expensive and more reliable connections between Ethernet/802.3 and token ring/802.5 LANs. In the routing area, both the OSI **IS/IS** and the Internet community's Open Shortest Path First (**OSPF**) standards are maturing into actual implementations. Both these standards are discussed in detail in *Mastering Advanced Internetworking*.

An Integrated Bridge Router

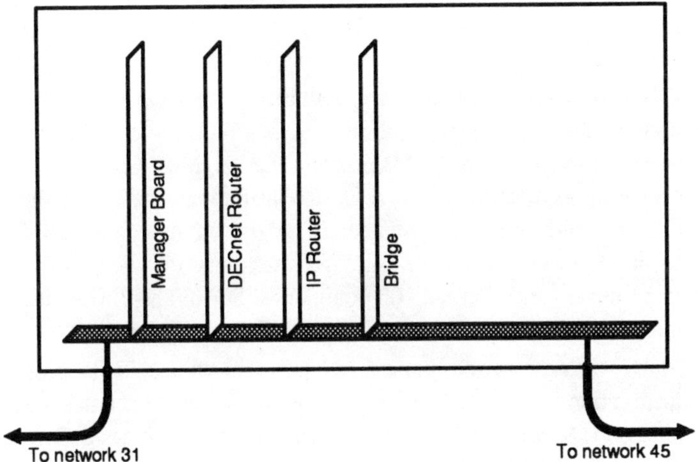

Future of LAN/WAN Integration

The most important WAN technologies and services are becoming more tightly integrated with LAN internet infrastructure devices.

- Traditional X.25 technology, including packet assembler/disassemblers (**PADs**) and X.25 gateways, is beginning to migrate to integrated bridge/routers.
- T-1 muxes are gaining routing capability just as T-1 and frame relay interfaces are appearing on advanced bridges and routers, in a two-way migration by LAN and WAN vendors.
- ISDN, SONET and SMDS are maturing into actual products. As imaging and video gain popularity, ISDN's H channels will become more attractive as pipes. SMDS is less mature. Most U.S. telcos are preparing to offer SMDS as a service tariffed similarily to today's Centrex, with "buy it as you need it" migration options. SONET is assuming more importance as a WAN backbone for telcos, government buyers and Fortune 100 companies. SONET's primary niche may be as a Metropolitan Area Network (MAN) choice.
- FDDI, already an important LAN protocol choice in its present incarnation in fiber, will become more popular as it becomes available on UTP and shielded twisted pair. This protocol has been purchased almost exclusively as a LAN and internet backbone; with a cheaper medium, FDDI is poised to make significant inroads as a to-the-desktop choice.

Finally, since the current separation of product types is more a function of who is selling into the LAN/internet market than it is a reflection of LAN users' real needs, whether or not vendors of communications products make significant inroads into the internetworking market will depend on how well they really understand and can respond to internet buyers' needs.

I strongly suggest that all internetwork designs be created in consultation with the end users and their managers, particularly when the internet includes a WAN. It seems clear that users whose real needs are not being served will ultimately rebel. In that kind of war, everyone loses.

How The Internet Technology Free-For-All May Sort Itself Out

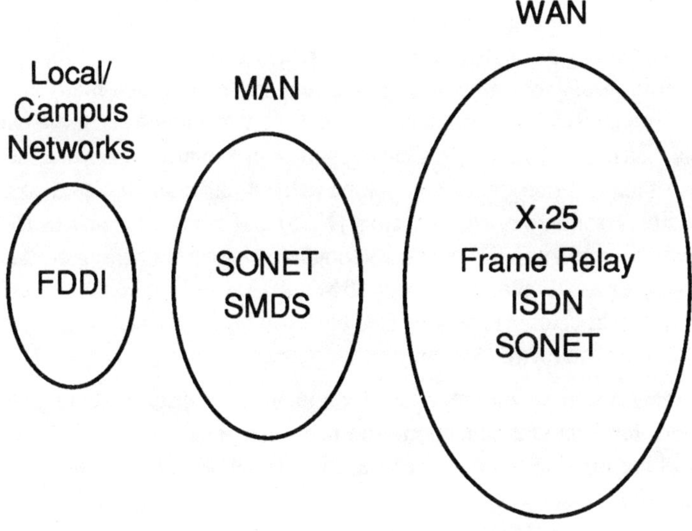

Customizing Your Future Training Plan

Your plans for additional training in networking technology and applications will undoubtedly depend on market trends and employment prospects in addition to personal interests and preferences. Obviously, a submarket that is expanding in the marketplace can support more employment and more job experimentation than a submarket that is stagnant, mature or even contracting.

Internetworking sales have been excellent through the start of the 1990s and will not start of level off until at least 1995. Sales should remain strong through the remainder of the decade, especially since the definition of "internetworking" will expand to embrace many new technologies. Within internetworking, bridge technology is more stable than router technology. Gateways come in so many flavors that they don't really represent a single submarket, but rather an unrelated composite of some very stable sectors (X.25) and other very new sectors (specific application gateways). Various enveloping/tunnelling product areas, especially those that allow IBM's SNA, DEC's DECnet or other major architectures to be traversed by newer protocols, can be grouped under thc "gateway" banner.

There is room on your needs list for both product-specific training and more fundamental education. Too many people spend most of their learning time on training because it will bring short-term benefits, as all quick-fix solutions do. Your company may encourage you to learn only those things that you can use on the job in the immediate future. For your long-term benefit, spend an equal amount of your time and money on education. The world is full of people who have learned a few buzzwords and key phrases but don't really understand what they mean. Don't be one of them. Your future is a structure you are building today and you can't build a sturdy structure on sand.

Balance Product Training With Education

Specific Training Examples	Education Examples
Using Vendor X's Network Management product	Network Management
Using Vendor Y's Protocol Analyzer	Architecture and Protocols
NOS #1 Network Engineering	Evolution of Network Operating Systems (NOSs)
Servicing Vendor W's Integrated Bridge/Router	Advanced Internetworking
Using Product G to create training	Theory of Instructional Design
Characteristics: Specific and narrow focus on "how"	Characteristics: In-depth understanding Broader focus on "why" and "what"

What Shall I Study? Where Can I Find It?

You will find university Extension and graduate degree programs of varying quality and length. This is generally a good and inexpensive place to start your education. Some vendors provide seminars in their subject area. These really vary in quality. At one end of the scale, Hewlett-Packard in the San Francisco Bay Area sponsors an excellent series of free, non-salesy seminars, for example. Specialized training companies are another potential source of information, especially for more state-of-the art technologies. If you can gather some colleagues with similar needs, try to get the university or one of the training vendors to provide you with an in-house seminar.

Books, audio tapes and videotapes are other sources to consider. The newspapers and magazines listed in Appendix B carry coupon ads for many of these training companies and book/audio/video companies. Finally, attendance at network conferences can usually be combined with tutorial days. These tutorials are usually very up-to-date; instructor quality varies.

Regarding subject area, consider

- more in-depth education in internetworking
- network management

This area is an excellent choice for future growth, but it has the least amount of available resources because it is such a new area.

- more in-depth education on high-level software

Server management and other Session/Presentation Layer software will become more important as the decade progresses. **Overlay software** is another interesting area to pursue for basic education.

Additional Education and Training

LAN Administrators	Telecom Administrators
1, 3, 5	1, 2, 8

MIS Analysts/Director	Internet Manager/Analyst
1-6, 8	1-7

Subject Areas

1. Local transport and wiring
2. WAN transport
3. High-level software
4. Network architectures and protocols
5. Network management
6. Advanced internetworking
7. High speed technologies
8. ISDN and voice/data

Investigate books, audio tapes, video tapes, University Extension, conference tutorials, professional organizations, training companies and vendors.

More Subject Areas for Education

Of course, the Physical Layer functions will always be an important area for study, as will basic architectures and transport. You may also consider

- More in-depth education on transport and wiring options

LAN vendors are primarily interested in selling LAN hubs, especially intelligent hubs. The increasing intelligence of hubs is a reflection of the need for more manageable networks and also the need for more cost containment. Hubs that can integrate ISDN with traditional LAN wiring and can also accommodate other new media and protocols (FDDI in particular) would be an excellent area for study. You can find classes in this area from local colleges and universities and from LAN vendors.

WAN transport is another area to investigate. Study opportunities include T-1/T-3, SONET, SMDS and the 802.6 MAN standard. These subjects will be most available at the more prestigious (well-funded) universities, from equipment vendors and telcos and from specialized training vendors.

- More in-depth education on network architectures

Client/server computing architectures will become more important components of your knowledge base as they become the dominant computing architecture.

Whatever subject area you decide to investigate in more detail and however you work at it, reward yourself for every step you take on the road to more knowledge. The true glory of living is to learn and grow. May you never stop.

Project: Chapter 6

Now that you have gained a greater understanding of internetwork technology, it's time to consider design or redesign of your internet infrastructure. Refer back to the inventory you completed in Chapter 1 and consider your options in light of your new knowledge.

- ❒ If you have no internet, how will you design it? Start with meetings with users and their managers, consider budgets, examine applications and traffic levels and don't rush the planning process.
- ❒ If you have an internet, how can you improve it?
  - What are the topology choices that you need to rethink?
  - How have user needs changed since the internet was installed?
  - Do you need new or different internet devices?
  - Do you need better or more extensive management tools?
- ❒ Examine your history files and talk to the managers about their business issues.
  - What are the core business applications that you have to protect?
  - How can you make the internet more of an asset and less of financial drain? (This is partially a matter of education. The internet may be delivering far more benefit than business managers realize.)

When you have a redesign or enhancement plan that you consider absolutely perfect, show it to one more person, preferably a trusted associate outside of your usual internal channels. It may be an external colleague. This final quality assurance step can have a dramatic impact on your final design.

Implement your new ideas and test their effectiveness. Keep thinking of ways to move the burden of repetitive or time-consuming labors to electronic servants. (For more ideas on internet management specifically, consult *Mastering Network Management* in this series.)

When you have successfully revamped your internet, raising corporate profits in the process, don't forget to take your hard-working and dedicated staff on a vacation. (If you don't have a hard-working and dedicated staff, you can take me.) Managing a network can be a grand adventure. Enjoy it!

Key Words

The words and phrases highlighted in **bold** represent key concepts in this chapter. Please take the time now to write down your own definitions of these terms, using the list below and additional paper if needed. Then compare your efforts to the training text. This is an excellent way for you to determine weak points in the breadth and depth of your understanding of this chapter.

RISC
IS/IS
OSPF
PADs
overlay software

7

'Tis A Puzzlement

The comprehensive final exam for this Internetworking course is a crossword puzzle. Don't panic! Crossword puzzles can be great fun. If you haven't completed a puzzle in a while, keep these hints in mind:

- Numbers are written out in words.
- Punctuation (dashes, for example) is ignored.
- If you think you have one answer figured out but it seems to preclude one or more other answers (pqw can't be an OSI Layer, can it?), think about the questions again. Sometimes you will see another way of approaching the question.
- Most importantly, go through the puzzle in its entirety once and fill in all the "easy" answers before you try the harder questions.

Enjoy!

Internetworking – The Puzzle

Down

1. Needs an "e"
2. Power source for bridges
3. Soothes a network manager's frazzled nerves with a "meow"
4. ST bridges do _____ bridging.
5. Bridge with a college education
6. Multi-Bus to DISOSS: an ______ gateway
7. Bridges and routers are (abbrev.) devices
8. Fractional, subrated and unsubrated are all options
12. 802 subcommittee number: network management
15. Internal Router (abbrev.)
17. Where engineers gather
20. Network manager's usual mien
21. Provides aspirin to cure 20 down
22. Bridge's response to a "foreign" address
25. Routers balance this
30. "_____ agead, spend as much as you want," the CFO said. The Network Manager fainted.

Across

2. Power source for routers
5. Frame that every device reads
9. Network status that makes managers smile
10. Frame-exchange layer
11. ATMs use this LAN application
13. When network managers eat lunch at their desk
14. Data _______ Layer
16. Routers are used as this kind of wall
18. How RIP measures "cost"
19. Routers listen for their _____________
23. Nice place to buy 8 Down equipment; HQ in Redwood City, CA
24. LAN vendors in the internet market sell ____-stop shopping
26. Second troubleshooting question: Is it ________?
27. Device must specify a complete path when using _______ routing
28. IEEE standards put a ______ between committee and sub committee numbers
29. 6 down gateway (abbrev.)
31. Internet managers need a can ____ attitude
32. Internet tree

See *Appendix A* for the solution to the puzzle.

Appendix A: Answer Keys

Chapter 0

1. b
2. d. Carrier sense multiple access with collision detect
3. physical, data link, network, transport, session, presentation and application
4. d
5. c. The rest are application programs, outside the OSI model.
6. a
7. c
8. b
9. d
10. e
11. c
12. a: Department of Defense; b: not a full stack, starts at third layer only; c: Telnet, not Telenet; d: the opposite is true.
13. b
14. c, because of security concerns. Too expensive for other applications now.
15. a
16. c
17. d
18. c
19. Check your definitions with a good LAN text.
20. Lower costs. Less education needed on each new product you buy. Products are evolutionary, not revolutionary; easier migration. Lower prices. Able to mix products from different vendors to get exactly what you need. Lower costs when doing business overseas (they use standards-based products).

21. Quicker to market with new products if basic platforms are standard. Lower manufacturing costs. Lower employee and customer training costs. Easier to find qualified employees. Less prospect education needed; sales cycle shorter. Small companies can poach on larger companies' customer base. Larger potential international market; can sell domestic products without much alteration.
22. d
23. b. They're on the same LAN.
24. Hint: UTP and STP are unshielded and shielded twisted pair wire.
25. You need both. The TCP/IP stack covers Layers 3-7. Ethernet covers Layers 1-2.
26. Put users closer to servers to improve response time and lower traffic levels. Make especially sure no bridges separate users and servers.
27. Security is a major concern. They are also easier to maintain and repair if they are kept in a single location; tools and spares inventory can be kept under control. Management staff costs are lower (less travel time). Servers cannot be damaged or compromised if acccss is limited.
28. Lower cost user platforms; lower cost server platforms relative to mainframes; faster response from distributed local dedicated servers; server focus on processing, users on display; more information is available in less time, etc. Request *Client/Server Computing* on Numidia Press response card.
29. c
30. a, NOT e.

Chapter 2

2. Data Link Source Address, Data Link Destination Address, Field Type, Data (which includes higher-layer control fields), Frame Check Sequence
3. Yes. Field Type
4. filter

5. dropped
6. learning; source
7. forward; flood
8. Looping. It creates a branching tree with a single root.
9. Source device, bridge or internet device
10. broadcasts, specific segment isolation, specific addresses, Network Layer protocol, length, etc.
11. Go/No Go, not interactive. Routing communication is interactive.

Chapter 3

Router Addressing Project:

Round 1: 30.235, 30.269, 37.382,129.101
Round 2: 201.314,201.311, 37.382,129.101
Round 3: 37.382,37.319, 37.382,129.101

Hybrid Internets Project:

Network 4590. Only bridges separate these two networks.

3. advertise
4. router-router communication.
5. topology
6. Hop count
7. ES/IS; IS/IS
8. an integrated bridge/router
9. second stand-alone router; add IP routing software to your existing router platform
10. Choose standards-based products
11. X.25 gateway
12. Either transforms structure of the packet or it simply envelopes the existing packet
13. If they use different, incompatible protocols.
14. envelope

15. If the server isn't very busy and you don't need much communications service. Add the two service levels together and make sure you aren't overtaxing your server's performance before you choose this option.
16. Where the business benefits of individual, immediate access to the WAN outweigh X.25 board costs. Stock and commodity brokers, international currency brokers, etc.

Chapter 4

1. High-bandwidth; digital; able to multiplex LAN and voice traffic; no-demand bandwidth allocation; etc.
2. Many remote locations with low overall traffic levels, most of which is focused on a central location. Branch offices connected to Headquarters, for example.
3. circuit
4. on demand
5. 64K; 56K; 8K
6. in
7 2.048 Mbps; 2.048 Mbps
8. 24
9. Low-error transmission lines; not delay-sensitive; end devices can handle error control
10. FECN; BECN; DE
11. DLCI
12. OC-1, OC-3

Chapter 5

1. Fault, configuration, performance, accounting, security.
5. Network interface Card (for a router port, for example): # of packets recieved, # of packets sent, # of collisions, # of TCP packets, # of IS packets; # of packet fragments, etc.

6. An architecture is a structure of interrelated functions - implemented in specific protocols - that puts all the specific protocols in a structured relationship with each other.
8. software
9. segment

Chapter 7

Appendix B: Publications, Conferences & Additional Reading

Publications

If you are not already receiving these publications, call and request a sample copy or visit your local technical bookstore:

Business Communications Review
Hinsdale, IL (800) 227-1234

Communications Week (weekly news)
Manhasset, NY (516) 562-5530

LAN (monthly)
San Francisco, CA (415) 905-2200

LAN Computing (monthly)
Horsham, PA

LAN Times
San Mateo, CA (415) 513-6800

Network Computing (monthly)
Manhasset, NY (516) 562-5071

Networking Management (monthly)
Westford, MA (508) 692-0700

Network World (weekly news)
Framingham, MA (508) 875-6400

In addition, *LAN Technology Magazine* focuses on the needs of systems integrators.

Conferences

There are dozens of good networking conferences every year, in the U.S. and abroad. The shows that focus most heavily on internetworking are the two Interop shows: on the west coast (San Francisco Bay Area) in October and in the District of Columbia area in April. Registration information is available at (415) 941-3399. NetWorld in Boston (Spring) and Dallas (Fall) are also excellent sources of ready-to-buy equipment information. Registration information is available through the Blenheim Group (201) 569-8542.

Additional Reading

For an in-depth, technical treatment of bridging and routing, I highly recommend Radia Perlman's (the mother of spanning tree) *Interconnections: Bridges and Routers*. For those of an engineering bent, Radia is a delight. One strong caveat for business readers: this author is very literate and articulate **for an engineer**. If plowing through 20 pages of tough technical explanations and then being told "Well, none of this stuff exists in products, but maybe it will some day and it's an interesting experiment if someone ever decides to do it" makes you livid over your wasted time and energy, or if you can't stomach naming your servers FOO, or if the *j* th instance of variable *v* makes you run screaming from the room, don't buy this book.

About The Author

Victoria Marney-Petix develops and delivers both live and computer-based training programs on network technology and management as Chief Consultant of Marpet Technical Services. In addition to local area networks and internetworking, her course list includes an in-depth look at networking architectures, a course on TCP/IP, an in-depth look at network management strategies and products, a course on ISDN designed especially for working network managers and a one-day seminar on high-speed networking options. She teaches at San Francisco State University Extension and the University of California Santa Cruz Extension.

Victoria also consults with vendors in the U.S. and Europe that are developing new network products and services, especially internet products, and with users who are managing complex internets.

Victoria's first book, *Networking and Data Communication* (1986, Prentice-Hall/Reston), received rave reviews in library publications, including ONLINE/Database magazine: *"I found myself so absorbed that I read the book in one sitting!... one of the best explanations of local area networks written to date."* Her second book, *Client/Server Computing*, was published in 1990.

Victoria has hosted several video training programs, most recently *Intro to LANs* and *Selling the Next Workstation*. In her non-networking life, Victoria is the producer/host of *Carrot Talk*, a weekly cable TV show focusing on care, behavior and training of pet rabbits. She spends 20 hours per week as a rabbit rescue volunteer.

You may contact the author directly at:

Marpet Technical Services
PO Box 2275
Fremont, CA 94536
(510) 792-9204

If you have comments on this book, please communicate with us (rather than the author) at **Numidia Press** by using the Comments form. We appreciate your feedback!

Comments

Title: **Mastering Internetworking**

Where did you buy this book?

- ❐ mail order
- ❐ bookstore (name) ______________________________
- ❐ employer (name) ______________________________
- ❐ training course ______________________________
- ❐ other (where?) ______________________________

I'd like you to know that: (tell us where we goofed, did a great job, could make improvements, left something out, etc.)

____

____

____

____

____

Tell us about yourself. Your name/address/phone is useful if we don't understand and need to call you to clarify, but you can remain incognito if you prefer. Your job title or function will help us to understand what kind of reader the problem impacts and this is important to us. An industry is equally helpful.

____

____

____

We appreciate all your help in making the next edition of this book even better than the present one. Thank you!

Numidia Press • P.O. Box 2281 • Fremont, CA 94536
Phone (510) 790-1199 • Fax (510) 797-5053

Cut Here

Fold here, staple or tape, stamp and mail

Place
Stamp
Here

Numidia Press
P.O. Box 2281
Fremont, CA 94536

Cut Here

Order Form

Please send me the books in the Self-Paced Learning Series:

_________ copies of *Mastering Internetworking* (**$24.95**)

_________ copies of *Mastering Advanced Internetworking* (**$24.95**)

_________ copies of *Mastering LAN Enabling Technologies* (10/93) (**$24.95**)

_________ Total number of books @ $24.95 each

_________ copies of *Alphabet Soup: Networking and Data Comm Acronyms* (**$8.95**)

$________ Subtotal

$________ CA addresses add $1.95 sales tax per book in Self-Paced Series and $.75 per *Alphabet Soup*

$________ Shipping (book rate: $1.50/book, air mail: $2.50/book)

$________ Amount enclosed

Discounts available on quantity & pre-pub orders!

Name ____

Company/Title ______________________________________

Address ____

City __________________________ State _______ Zip ___________

Full money-back guarantee!

❐ Please send me a catalog of books and videos available from Numidia Press

Please make check payable to

Numidia Press
P.O. Box 2281
Fremont, CA 94536
(510) 790-1199

Cut Here

Fold here, staple or tape, stamp and mail

Place
Stamp
Here

Numidia Press
P.O. Box 2281
Fremont, CA 94536

Cut Here

Index